Praise for

KEEPING KATHERINE

"Susan Zimmermann's deeply moving book about her child Katherine is one that will touch all people, not only parents. Her courage, her joy, and her hope reach through her tragedy and offer us all a way of life that is creative, no matter what the circumstances."

       Madeleine L'Engle, Newbery Award–winning author

"Here is a journey into the deepest center of the soul. Susan Zimmermann portrays, with honesty, passion and wisdom, a chapter of her life that is both deeply terrifying and wholly inspiring. It is a story of loss, pain, joy, and—above all—profound truth. It is a story with the power to change your life."

       T.A. Barron, author of The Lost Years of Merlin

"Susan Zimmermann has written a book about her daughter, but also a book about each of us—the fragile, damaged, but insistently precious part deep inside, that refuses to be cast off. To read these pages is to be reminded of the value of life itself. I have rarely been so moved."

       Swanee Hunt, former U.S. Ambassador to Austria

"Susan's story—and Kat's—turned out to be a profound gift to me. I had expected 'heavy' reading—difficult and depressing. I found instead a love story. Susan reminds us that it isn't what happens to us that determines our life, but how we respond to it."

       Marilyn Van Derbur, author of Miss America by Day

KEEPING KATHERINE

A Mother's
Journey to Acceptance

SUSAN ZIMMERMANN

THREE RIVERS PRESS
NEW YORK

Published by Three Rivers Press, New York, New York.
Member of the Crown Publishing Group, a division of Random House, Inc.
www.crownpublishing.com

Originally published in slightly different form by Nemo Press in 1996.

THREE RIVERS PRESS and the Tugboat design are
registered trademarks of Random House, Inc.

Printed in the United States of America

Design by Meryl Sussman Levavi

Library of Congress Cataloging-in-Publication Data is available on request.

ISBN 1-4000-5201-7

10 9 8 7 6 5 4 3 2 1

First Edition

To Katherine, my teacher

ACKNOWLEDGMENTS

Always and forever, my thanks

to Paul Phillips, my husband of thirty years, who has walked each step of this journey with me, who steadfastly believed in the power and importance of Katherine's story, and whose prowess as an editor is simply colossal;

to Helen, Alice, and Mark, who in their grade-school years gave me the space and encouragement to "keep writing, Mom," and who always treated their big sister Kat with kindness, love, and acceptance;

to my father and mother, Keith and Mary Jane Zimmermann, who taught me all I know about resilience and carrying on no matter what the obstacles;

to Paul Phillips Sr. and Rita, whose unconditional love of and delight in Katherine helped me understand that I, too, could celebrate Katherine as she is;

to Donna Bell, Katherine's companion and best friend, whose spirit of adventure and goodness opened my eyes to the potential Kat holds;

to Faye Bender, my agent, who believed in my writing and this book enough to make sure *Grief Dancers* got reincarnated as *Keeping Katherine;*

to many dear friends—Kate Adams, T. A. Barron, Sharon Bush, Stephen Cunningham, Wendell Fleming, Lorrie Grillo, Mike Keefe, Madelyn Kershner, Frank and Linda Plaut, Paul Reville, Francie Thompson, Rosa Venezia—who read early drafts, indulged my need for feedback, and gave me invaluable advice;

to Kathy Hunter and my friends at the International Rett Syndrome Association, whose devotion to unraveling the mysteries of Rett syndrome will lead someday to a cure;

to Katherine for being my Katherine.

The world is indeed full of peril, and in it there are many dark places; but still there is much that is fair, and though in all lands love is now mingled with grief, it grows perhaps the greater.

J. R. R. Tolkien,
The Lord of the Rings

PROLOGUE

Katherine, age 11.

We are our stories. Our stories give meaning to our lives. Through them, we discover ourselves. By sharing them, they give us strength and make us part of something larger that embraces all the mysteries of life's joys and sorrows.

EARLY IN THE MORNING, I sit looking out to the dark silhouette of the Continental Divide. I sip my morning coffee, holding the large flowered mug to warm my hands. My terry cloth robe wraps around my legs. The wind chimes play their high-pitched song. The old clock, a hand-me-down from my grandfather Nemo, ticks away on the mantel. In the background I hear Katherine's sounds but know I don't need to go to her yet. The other children sleep. Paul dreams. Soon I will turn on the light and write again about my life with Katherine.

Katherine turned my world upside down. For years, I struggled to put together the fragments of the shattered dream and to ease the pain of living with my profoundly handicapped child. For too long, I found only dissonance and confusion in her presence. I was unable to listen to her silence.

Only when I went back and retrieved the images from the past that haunted me, when I let the pain, anger, and loneliness out on the page, when I spent hours holding Katherine, letting her hushed messages through my skin and into my heart, could I get to a point of accepting her and finding the beauty in her crippled body.

This is a book about writing through grief. It is a book about doing what we think we cannot do. It is a story about our powers to heal ourselves. It is a story about the strength of family and community. And it is a story about the need we have to take our sorrows and our losses and find a way to move through them. By confronting and enduring despair and darkness, by not looking away, we allow the experience of grief to transform us and we are able to transform the pain into the expression of our very souls.

Throughout, I include in italics brief musings that capture the perspective gained and lessons learned through the struggle of keeping Katherine always with us, a touchstone to what is important and a reminder of the power of the powerless.

KEEPING
KATHERINE

CHAPTER 1

Paul and Susan on their wedding day, May 25, 1974.

Our stories shape us. They give us our songs and our silence. When they are full of joy, they allow us to soar. When they are full of pain, they allow us to journey into the darkness of our souls where we meet ourselves, sometimes for the first time. They destroy us and allow us to rebuild. We must share our stories. They are our gifts.

BEFORE DAWN on September 2, 1979, contractions began. I lay in bed with three pillows piled under my legs and drank hot tea. Paul brought me a bowl of honeydew and ran a bath. I sucked the juice from the melon. Maybe it's false labor, I thought. The baby's due date was two weeks away. I had just turned twenty-eight. I'd been married for five years.

I soaked in the old tub with ornate feet and took deep, slow breaths. Leaning back, I rubbed my hands across my tight belly and thought about the child I didn't know, but already adored.

Six years earlier, Paul had spotted me across the aisle in the Yale Law Library, during our first month of law school. I sat, wearing overalls and a T-shirt, with one leg slung over the arm of the chair and my face buried in a book. My dark hair curled short around my head. I looked like a country kid visiting the city and probably seemed young and naïve compared to many of the students who, unlike me, actually wanted to be lawyers. I dove into law school but never knew quite why I was there or where it would lead.

I'd gone to Woodsfield High School, a small school in southeastern Ohio. The French teacher didn't speak French. Band, football, and cheerleading took priority over academics. I'd gone on to college at Chapel Hill in North Carolina, where I'd done well, but Yale was different.

Students seemed to talk and think faster. Many already had law firm résumés and big plans for their futures.

When I started at Yale, my dad took me aside and said, "Susan, there will be a lot of people there who are smarter than you, more brilliant, better educated. You can make up for a lot with plain hard work. If you plan on ninety-nine percent perspiration and one percent inspiration, you'll do fine."

One day early in the fall of 1973, I walked through the main corridor in sweat clothes. Paul stopped me and asked if I'd like to run. We headed out Prospect Street past the Forestry and Divinity Schools to Whitney Avenue.

At first I viewed him as a friend and running partner, nothing more. When I entered his dorm room, Bach or Vivaldi played in the background. He wore thick black glasses and had a Charlie Chaplin mustache. He went to church on Sundays and spent his spare time reading G. K. Chesterton and Samuel Johnson. He'd gone to a Catholic military school in D.C. and on to Harvard. One hot day, after a long run together, he grabbed the end of his T-shirt, took off his glasses, and wiped the sweat from his eyes. I began to fall in love with him in that brief moment before he put his glasses back on, as he squinted blindly, revealing an unexpected vulnerability.

The following May, with baroque music playing, we were married in Yale's Dwight Memorial Chapel, a small

Gothic church with well-scuffed wooden floors, stone walls, and stained-glass windows. I wore a veil of Belgian lace from Paul's grandmother and carried one long-stemmed white rose.

The summer after we married, Paul and I lived in D.C. and worked at U.S. Customs writing legal opinions on how U.S. tariffs applied to a bizarre array of imported goods. Every morning, we bicycled to work, a seven-mile route that wound through Rock Creek Park and past the D.C. zoo. It gave us a fresh start to the day. Paul insisted I wear a motorcycle helmet—a heavy black thing with red lightning strikes on the sides. Paul wore a hockey helmet with a lot more ventilation. By late afternoon, when we trekked home, every cool breath had died. Car exhausts puffed. Heat lay over the city like a hairnet. I rode irritated by the commuters who pointed at me from their air-conditioned cars, feeling like I had a sauna on my head. Most days, by the time we got to the house, I had a headache and a bad attitude.

It was a tug-of-war summer. We were in love, but also strong-willed, which made the necessary compromises of marriage difficult. There was an up-and-down quality to time. The morning bike rides were our daily dose of freshness. The evening rides brought out the tensions.

After graduating from law school in 1976, the Rockies and sunshine drew us back to Denver, where Paul and I had spent a previous summer as law clerks. We worked at downtown firms and spent many weekends bagging peaks in the high country.

Paul hiked for the sheer adventure. He liked to bushwhack as much as I liked a trail. He always searched for circle routes and never minded rambling around for half a day. For me, there were too many "circle routes to nowhere," but Paul always got us home safely.

Our house sat across the street from Mercy Hospital, near City Park. A steady stream of hookers worked Colfax Avenue a block away. Houses that had been renovated to pristine condition stood next to places that had torn sofas on their front porches.

Mercy Hospital's parking lot was out our front door. Paul built a white picket fence to hide the parking-lot view and erected a six-foot fence around our postage-stamp-sized backyard. We painted the interior "Navajo white" from basement to attic, ripped up the green shag carpet, and toted railroad ties and flagstone to build patios and vegetable gardens. For weeks, we scrounged lower downtown for old bricks to add inexpensive character to our landscaping. This was how we built our life as a young married couple, before Katherine.

The warm water didn't soothe the contractions away. Leaning back in the tub, I closed my eyes and practiced Lamaze breathing. I ran more hot water so only the top of my belly broke the surface. I dreaded the pain that was to come, certain that at the critical moment I'd forget the right breathing technique. I wanted more time to clean the house and get the baby's room ready.

That Sunday morning, we walked the short distance through the parking lot to Mercy Hospital. The first few hours passed uneventfully; then the contractions came closer. After hours of pushing, the baby wouldn't come out. Finally, the doctor used forceps. There were no marks.

With Katherine's first cry, I felt a new dimension. My life would be forever deepened. My body shook from the strain of three hours of pushing. Blood vessels throughout my face had burst. The doctor held her up covered with mucus. Never had I seen anything so hideously beautiful. Then they wiped her clean and gently placed her in my arms.

Katherine Rose, an elegant name full of history and power: Katherine—an old family name, the name of queens; and Rose—for Ruzicka, Rose in Czech, Paul's mother's maiden name. When we first put the names together, we stopped looking. We had the name. Our Katherine Rose would blossom into a glorious flower.

By this time Paul's parents, Paul Sr. and Rita, had left D.C. and retired to Colorado. They rushed down from their nearby home in Winter Park to meet Katherine. Paul Sr. stood holding her awkwardly and stared at her delicate features. "I've never seen a lovelier creature," he said. Rita wrapped Katherine in soft pink blankets, sat in the tan hospital chair with metal arms, and began a conversation that was to last for years.

It was clear to me that I had been waiting for Katherine all my life. The connection went beyond words to a place I'd never known. She gave me the joy of complete and uncomplicated love—a love that grew stronger with each diaper change and midnight feeding.

Every morning Paul and I brought her into bed with us. Her broad smiles and playful chortles remain imprinted on my mind. Her early "Mamas" and "Dadas" still ring in my head.

I took a break from work. Returning to corporate law now held little appeal. I headed a project to plant trees in our neighborhood, joined a babysitting co-op, and watched as Kat grew. She learned to sit and say a few words. She played with the activity center attached to her crib, making it clang and whir like any baby would. She greeted me with outstretched arms and laughter. In her baby book, I wrote: "How Katherine laughs when you make funny noises at her or blow on her tummy. She is delighted when she is left sitting up and playing with her toys. She is thrilled by splashing and kicking in the tub, but her blue doll brings her more joy than anything else."

When Kat was seven months old, I found a part-time job working for the state Department of Regulatory

Agencies. The work was interesting but not overly demand-
ing—a perfect balance, three workdays, four days with
Katherine.

Several months later, I stopped writing in Katherine's
baby book. I told myself I was too busy. Much later, I realized the small landmarks of her progress were no longer
there to be charted.

*When do we first know our lives are forever changed? When
do our hearts sink to our stomachs, our breaths catch in our
throats, our bodies turn leaden? What do we do when we
know there is nothing we can do?*

CHAPTER 2

Susan and Katherine, spring 1980.

How do I speak of the pain now, when fifteen years have passed? How do I talk about the gulf that grew between Paul and me? How do I go back, when I let a part of myself remain numb for so long? When I began writing about the images I'd buried so deeply, a flood of tears burst forth, drenching my heart and soul, allowing the healing to begin.

KAT DRANK the water. It looked pure and fresh. We had no idea how much we would come to regret that innocent drink.

When Katherine was eleven months old, we backpacked in Colorado's Collegiate Range with our friends Luke and Rosa. We had clear skies as Kat and her floppy blue doll traveled to alpine meadows on my back. The second day out, we stopped for a picnic near a mountain stream. We sat in mountain grasses chasing butterflies with our hands. Paul scooped water from the stream and gave it to Kat to drink with her banana. She grabbed the aluminum cup and drank, spilling water all over her doll and overalls. I took several large gulps as I ate my cheese sandwich. We were high up, where water came from snowmelt. Paul didn't use purification pills.

Soon after that trip, I became ill. My body ached and I felt dizzy when I stood. I continued nursing Katherine, not thinking much of it. After several days, my fever crept over 104 degrees Fahrenheit.

I spent a week in the hospital with a high fever and a splitting headache, drifting in and out of sleep. After administering scores of tests, the doctors couldn't diagnose the illness, but I knew it was the water that had made me ill.

That week I weaned Katherine, cutting out the morning and evening breast-feedings I'd never wanted to end.

I stopped reluctantly—too sick to keep on and afraid of what I might pass to her.

Mother came out to help. Every day she brought Katherine to visit. Kat sat at the end of my hospital bed full of giggles and smiles as she tossed her blue doll in the air. My daytime nurse told me how lucky I was to have Katherine. "She's a living doll," she said and then told me about her seven-year-old son who had cerebral palsy. "It happened at birth. We never knew what went wrong." She pulled from her wallet a picture of a thin blond child lying over a huge, multicolored ball with a smile lighting his face. His beauty and his mother's love for him struck me, but at that point in my life I could muster only detached sympathy.

Finally, my fever broke. The hospital released me the day before Kat turned one. A cousin with a daughter Kat's age invited us to celebrate together. By then her daughter was walking and climbing all over furniture. Kat had just learned to get from her stomach to a sitting position.

In photos from that first birthday party, Kat wears a dark-blue dress with red smocking, white tights, and white leather shoes. Her hair is cut chin length. She looks like an old-fashioned doll with big eyes and chubby cheeks. In every picture, she clutches a toy or stuffs cake in her mouth.

Mother and I sat in my kitchen. I still felt weak and light-headed from the illness. Katherine grabbed chunks of a peanut butter and jelly sandwich off the tray of her high chair. A window fan circulated the hot September air. Mother sipped instant coffee. She watched Katherine too closely. I acted as if I didn't notice. "Why isn't she standing, pushing up on furniture? She's a year old. She seems slow, Sue."

A lump settled in my stomach. I quickly told her everything Kat could do. "She says Mommy and Daddy. She picks up Cheerios. She moves all over the place on her tummy. She smiles, laughs, greets us."

I took her in for a one-year checkup. Her pediatrician said everything looked fine. "Don't worry about the delay. She's well within the curve."

Later that month, we visited my parents in New Haven. After a weekend in New York, Paul stayed in the city for business and I returned alone to New Haven by train to be with Katherine. On the ride back, I couldn't read. I couldn't concentrate. I had an ominous sense I needed to get back to Katherine as quickly as possible.

Down the corridor in the New Haven station, I saw a baby sitting on a middle-aged woman's lap. The child wore pink overalls and a white turtleneck and had pink bows in her dark hair. Candy wrappers littered the floor. A crowd pushed its way out of the dingy station to waiting cars.

I saw her from a distance and thought, "What a pretty child." As I got closer, I noticed her body slumped. Her head drooped over her chest. She didn't make eye contact. Her eyes crossed. She looked around but didn't focus. A shiver ran down my spine when I realized it was Katherine sitting on Mother's lap.

In dreams, this image finds me: my first view of Katherine as a hurt child. In the dreams I don't know who the woman and child are. I have to walk very near the orange plastic chair to recognize them.

When I was little, Mother smelled of cinnamon and Jergens lotion. Her body wrapped around me soft and warm as I cuddled on her lap. Night after night, she scratched my back, massaged the growing pains out of my legs, and put a hot-water bottle at my feet. If I needed a hug or a talk or a companion, I knew where to go.

In my memory, Mother sits in a wingback chair, talking as her needles work wool into sweaters with cables and designs. I sit on the floor beside her, my hands struggling to control the unwieldy spears, trying to match her grace and ease, but losing loops of yarn. I knot over the mistakes, proud when I finish a line. Mother, when she sees the imperfections, takes the needles gently from me and tears out the work to the place before the gaps. I falter as her needles dance circles with the wool.

She sits at the sewing machine, making drapes for a house we will soon leave. She stands in the background as we play with friends, half in shadows watching from a distance, allowing us to make mistakes but ready to swoop down immediately to save us from real harm.

Mother's life revolved around the warm nests she created time and again as Dad was transferred and the family uprooted. Wherever we put down shallow roots, she made a home of fine curtains and plush carpets.

Once Mother saw something was wrong with Katherine, she held her less and seemed to have a hard time looking at her. She kept frantically telling us Katherine wasn't normal, perhaps desperate for us to do something to help Kat. Paul and I shook our heads in disbelief.

"I'm right, Sue. There's something wrong with that child," Mother would say. I'd stand nearby with "no, no, no" going through my head.

Mother kept making sweaters and smocked dresses for Katherine, but it was as if she closed a window in her mind. She could look through it, but she couldn't reach out to embrace Katherine. For the first time in my life, I felt abandoned, like a child cast out to sea on a boat with no compass and no oars. Later, I realized that Mom was unable to deal with a less-than-perfect grandchild. Mother, the doting grandmother, couldn't bear to admit her own helplessness. She couldn't make Katherine right. She couldn't be there for me.

Dad stood in the background, acting as if nothing was happening. He never asked me how Katherine was doing or how I was doing.

Soon after my trip to New Haven, I had a long talk with
a friend at the office. She said whenever she had a tough
problem, she wrote about it in her journal for three weeks.
By the end of that time, it had gone away. I began keeping a journal, believing if it worked for her, it would work
for me.

> OCTOBER 2, 1980, JOURNAL ENTRY
> For the past few weeks, our thoughts have been muddy
> and heavy. Katherine seems different. She is not as
> playful and inquisitive. At times, she doesn't seem to
> recognize us. She cries more for no apparent reason.
> She crosses her eyes and sucks her thumb. She always
> seems tired. I'm terribly puzzled. Something has
> changed, but I have no idea what or why. On the trip
> to New Haven, she seemed like a different child.
> Where are the smiles and looks of recognition?

Around this time, Katherine began running a low-
level fever she couldn't shake. I feared I'd passed my illness to her in breast milk, or she, too, had been infected by
the stream water. Over and over, I told myself, if I can get
better so can she.

We took her in for tests. "We know some of the best
doctors in town," Paul said. "They'll find answers and
have Katherine well in no time."

One doctor teased about the eye crossing. "She's going through a stage she'll grow out of. Right now, playing with her eyes amuses her." Another told us she looked like a Gerber baby and said we were overanxious parents.

At first, I was relieved by such remarks. As the weeks passed and Katherine retreated deeper into her shell, I felt like a child running to get help for a drowning friend and being stopped by adults who would say, "Honey, we're busy right now. Don't interrupt." Inside I screamed, "Don't you see she's slipping away? Can't you do something?"

Our anxiety evolved from concern to fear to terror. "Paul, she didn't have time to build up her immunities. What I could fight, maybe she can't." The helplessness sank in and with it a silent anger at Paul. At some level, I blamed his childish exuberance for the dire situation in which we found ourselves. In the wilderness, his playful side is in full swing. Because the stream looked clean and benign rippling over the boulders, he didn't slow down and think. Normally cautious, he'd made the biggest mistake of his life. Now I was the one picking up the pieces, taking Katherine from one doctor to the other, while he put in long hours as a lowly associate at a big law firm. He could escape. I couldn't.

Gradually, she stopped greeting us. She stopped saying "Mama" and "Dada." She stopped putting her arms up for me to hold her. There was an unreal quality to time—as if we were surrounded by fog watching a train crash in slow motion. The train steered toward disaster, but nothing could be done to change its course.

When did my love for Paul mingle with hate? When did the anger erupt? When did the pain, like a tick, dig deep into my soul? How did I deal with the horror of my husband destroying my only child? A cacophony of confusion: hate/love, anger/compassion, togetherness/distance, hope/helplessness, all wrapped in despair.

Kat sat in the middle of the living room on the Chinese carpet bordered with purple iris and maroon peacocks. She swayed back and forth, wringing her hands, turning around and around, her bottom the fulcrum, her foot the lever. Toys lay about her, my pathetic effort to give her the opportunity to reach out and be normal.

In her crib she still had the activity center. Before, she'd spent long periods playing with it. In the early mornings then, I'd hear the clang of bells and the whir of the multicolored wheel; the activity center, our wake-up call. I loved that toy. The day we received it—a late baby present—I attached it to the crib's side rungs and waited in anticipation for Kat to make its whistles and bells come alive. First, she kicked the brightly colored wheel with her foot. Soon after, she pushed the plastic lever that made a loud scratchy sound. Within a couple of months, she brought the activity center to life whenever she was in her crib. Mobiles and a bunny music box were attached nearby. It was the activity center that captured her imagination.

But things changed. Each morning I waited anxiously for the sounds. I stood outside Kat's room and held my breath, thinking if I could hold it long enough she'd start playing with the activity center again. Occasionally she bumped into it and I thought she had resumed her passion, but I never again heard her make music with its bells and levers. Day after day, the activity center sat untouched in her crib.

One morning I found Kat silent, awake in her crib, sitting, putting her hands in her mouth, and crossing her eyes. With tears streaming down my face, I unscrewed the activity center and stored it in the closet. I left Katherine in her crib and sat in the corner of my room with my face buried in my hands.

My friend Rosa, who'd been with Paul and me on the camping trip, drove over from Boulder, bringing a fresh peach pie. Rosa's thick black hair hung to her shoulders in a graceful pageboy. Her bangs cut straight across her forehead, shading green eyes and exotic features. She wore white pants, an oversized sweater, and Birkenstocks with wool socks.

Rosa and I sat at the table in my yellow kitchen and drank mint tea as the pie heated. It was the first time a freshly baked pie had been in my oven. The sweet smell of peaches filled the room as I told Rosa about the changes we'd seen in Katherine, trying to act as if it were no big deal. The fear and loneliness stuck in my throat. I broke down.

"Rosa, she drank the water. It's all because of that drink. I don't know what to do. We're losing her."

Rosa stroked my back until finally her presence and the smell of peaches calmed me. We took turns feeding Kat, then taking bites ourselves. Peach juice trickled down our chins. Katherine giggled. After the pie, Rosa held Kat in our Victorian rocker and hummed old blues songs in her deep voice until Kat fell asleep.

CHAPTER 3

PHOTO BY SUSAN ZIMMERMANN

Paul and Katherine, spring 1980.

We are a fix-it culture, a culture that thinks we are masters of our environment. We are proud and in control. We find it almost impossible to accept those gray areas where there are no answers, no clues—just mystery.

I SPENT HOURS in our dining room with early pictures of Katherine spread across the table, searching for a sign that would tell us what was happening. The photos showed her smiling, playing with toys, hugging Paul and me. I carefully put together an album of those pictures to carry with me to the hospitals. If I showed the doctors how normal she'd been, maybe they would try harder to fix her.

During a three-day stay at Children's Hospital, more than twenty different doctors examined her. One pediatric neurologist said her behavior—the lethargy, the eye crossing, the fever—fit a viral encephalitis diagnosis. It was the first time I'd heard encephalitis as a possibility.

"She could have gotten it from the water, or from the mosquitoes," he said, less baffled by the eye crossing than other doctors had been. "I've seen it before. Retardation is unlikely because of her normal development in her first year. I've seen children much worse than Katherine recover completely."

When I told Paul, he held me tight and we started laughing in relief.

"All right!" he said. "It's going to be fine, Sue. Kat will come back to us. You'll see."

We went to the library. Paul brought me thick medical treatises as I sat at the wooden table. We deciphered enough of the medical lingo to understand viral encephalitis was an inflammation of the brain caused by a virus.

A slow recovery was typical. Brain damage could result, but even desperately ill patients sometimes recovered completely.

Other doctors at Children's stressed they didn't really know what the problem was. No test could be run that positively confirmed the encephalitis. But the only words I truly heard were those of the pediatric neurologist that gave me a glimmer of hope.

Our pediatrician recommended more tests. We spent three days at Colorado General, a teaching hospital with more testing facilities. Teams of doctors and medical students came into the room to examine Katherine. Kat sat in the corner of the crib, leaning against its high metal bars. She crossed her eyes and swayed back and forth. Around her, a group of men in white coats stood talking about her as if she weren't there. I wanted her to smile and charm them, but she withdrew further into herself. I pulled out the photo album.

"Here's what she was like just a few months ago," I said, pointing at a picture of Katherine hugging her blue doll, an animated look on her face. They kept looking at the Katherine in the crib.

They poked Kat for vials of blood, hooked her up to an EKG, taped on a twenty-four-hour urine bag, did a CAT scan, tapped her spine for fluid, did an ultrasound for the heart, and conducted an ophthalmological exam. I held her down as she screamed and fought the needles.

With each test, something in me died. I wasn't a good mother. I didn't deserve to be a mother at all. Any decent mother would keep her child safe from all of these intrusions.

At night Katherine was up until after midnight crying. I stayed in the empty bed next to hers. I brought her into my bed and held her against me, stroking her back and humming lullabies. Nothing soothed her. Every couple of hours, nurses came in to check her, banging around, waking us as we drifted off.

When we left Colorado General, the doctors told us all the test results were normal. They didn't know what was wrong with Katherine. They agreed encephalitis could have caused the problem, but there had been no definitive test results. With no definite diagnosis, there was no treatment. All we could do was wait and see.

I walked away with the beeps of thermometers, the smells of disinfectant, the sounds of Katherine's cries, the ring of metal crib bars clanging like a prison door in my head, and a horrible sense that Kat was innocent but she'd been sentenced for life and there was nothing I could do to change it.

Kat continued her downward spiral. We moved to a new house in a new neighborhood. The master bedroom was huge. But it was the sunroom, perfect for a nursery, that had sold us on 730 Josephine—an old-fashioned redbrick house located on a one-way street in one of Denver's downtown neighborhoods.

We first saw 730 Josephine when Katherine was nine months old, and we imagined her playing in that sun-filled room. The nursery had paned windows on three sides that let light pour into it. We bought a white fluffy rug, painted the room white, bought a white wicker rocking chair, and put Kat's white crib under the bright windows on the north side. At first she slept in the nursery. It suited her. It was as pretty as she was.

Then the crying started and never ended. In the middle of the night, Kat cried like a child lost in a dark forest. It was as if her head hurt and the throbbing wouldn't stop. I brought her into our bed night after night. Rarely could I soothe her. I dreaded the nights. I spent the days in a fog watching Kat's every move, knowing her hands weren't working and her eyes crossed, yet marking each fleeting sign of normalcy. I believed in her in the daylight.

At night it was much harder to believe. No radio talked in the background. No phone broke the stillness. No distractions disturbed the mind's focus. A baby's scream was like a foghorn—loud and haunting in a minor key.

Kat cried and cried. I hated it and I began to hate her. I slept fitfully. Night after night, I lay awake listening to her screams, knowing a mother's touch couldn't work its magic and wondering why she was doing this to me. At night, I blamed Kat. No longer was she an innocent child, but a curse sent to destroy my life. How could I keep up with the routine of doctors, hospitals, and sleepless nights? How long would it be before the bleakness of the night crept into every waking hour?

One day I set up a crib downstairs—one of those fold-up playpens, the type I vowed I'd never cage my child in. I couldn't spend another helpless night listening to her sobs.

"Sue, do you really need to do that?" Paul asked. "That's her room."

"I can't sleep. It's driving me crazy. How can you sleep through it?" I asked.

The first night I put Kat down there, I felt I was giving my child away. I didn't know what was happening to her. I just knew there was nothing I could do about it and that I couldn't bear one more night. Her brain was turning against her. She struggled to retain some link to this world, but couldn't hang on.

The year 1981 dawned cold and dark. Katherine was sixteen months old. I was tired all the time and lived a roller-coaster life of heights and dips, the dips grimmer because of the heights when hope filled my heart.

Kat woke at 5:00 every morning in the darkness. I heard her clucking sounds and cries and knew she was chewing her hands, fading to some distant world.

Paul slept beside me as I lay in bed, wishing Katherine were not a part of my life, fearing the worst and wanting to leave it all behind, but having no idea where I would go. Paul woke. We avoided each other's eyes, too familiar with the haunted, scared looks. Our fears grew. But we couldn't talk about them. I think we both felt that if we gave words to our thoughts, we'd jinx everything, dooming Katherine's future and our own. Paul tried to be cheerful, rushing downstairs for coffee.

I slipped down to check on Kat. He'd soon come in, coffee cups in hand, and find me staring at the ceiling.

"She didn't even recognize me this morning," I'd say. "Nothing."

We'd sit side by side in the dark bedroom, silent with our shared fear and sadness, letting the coffee do its work.

Other days, I'd approach the crib and find Katherine smiling, reaching her arms up to me. A rush of joy and love would surge through me as I carried her off to our bed to show Paul. We'd place her between us, certain she would come back to us, that we'd win in the end, that we'd awaken from the bad dream, and all would be as it had been that first year.

I'd dress Kat in a hand-smocked dress or velour outfit, hoping her pretty face and pretty clothes would somehow banish her vacant look. Then Paul fed her breakfast while I rushed out for early runs down Seventh Avenue, past the grand houses and neat landscaping. I nodded to the other joggers and wondered what their lives were like, whether they, too, were trying to run some pain away.

Three days a week, I worked at the Colorado Department of Regulatory Agencies. A cousin babysat for Katherine while I worked. It was a relief to get out of the house, but once I was at my desk, the worry began.

At home I'd sit on a low leather sofa in the den, watching Katherine, desperately hoping for signs of improvement, but seeing all too clearly that she was drifting even further away. At times she tensed her whole body, tossing her head and rolling her eyes back. She clenched her fists. Her hands and feet had a purplish tint and were very cold. She rarely used her hands now, almost never to pick up either food or a toy.

In February, I had slight stomach cramps and unusual fatigue. A home pregnancy test confirmed my hunch. I spent that morning in a daze, one moment thinking it was the worst thing that could have happened, the next thinking it was the best.

I called Paul at the office. "You won't believe this. I'm pregnant. Paul, did you hear me?"

"Sue, you don't mean it. How can we handle another child right now?"

"It'll be okay," I said, not at all sure it would be.

"But, Sue, you're a wreck. We're both wrecks. What about taking care of Kat? The timing couldn't be worse."

"It might be good for her to have someone to play with. It might help her and us."

At nineteen months, Kat wasn't walking or crawling. She moved around, sometimes in an awkward crawl position, but always haphazardly, as if she didn't know where she was going.

During this period, she got sick a lot. When she didn't have a high fever, she had a low-grade one. I kept thinking if she could only get healthy, maybe then she'd have a chance. She lay in bed sucking her hands and crossing her eyes. With each virus, she seemed more withdrawn. I lived in a murky limbo, not sure about anything involving Kat's diagnosis. I blamed the perpetual colds, holding to the belief that she would recover from the encephalitis once she got over them. Yet in the mornings I'd wake and feel an icy grip tightening on my heart, because I had an inkling that I was never going to get my Katherine back.

I took Katherine to Children's Hospital three mornings a week for physical and occupational therapy and worked for hours with her on the exercises at home. I took her to a speech therapist at the University of Denver. I had, by then, given up on doctors and hospitals. They had no answers for us. They couldn't break into Katherine's shell or give us any sense of her future.

How do we know when it is time to let go of our dreams and embrace our lives as they are? When do we stop hoping and simply accept? When can we say: I have not been defeated, I have triumphed; I have moved to a place beyond hope?

CHAPTER 4

Katherine, age 2, 1981.

Sometimes we need to retreat to a soundproof room. We need to go deep within ourselves where nothing can get through. We need to close out all distractions and go to a place so empty and remote that not another person on this earth can find us. We need to allow ourselves the terror of confronting the shadow of our souls. Maybe we will back away, not yet ready, unable to do anything but lean against padded walls.

THAT SPRING I dressed Katherine in her prettiest dresses, smoothed her hair, held it back with butterfly barrettes, and took pictures. I posed her carefully and waited until the grimaces had passed to push the button. I'd pick up the photos at the grocery store. Before, I always opened pictures immediately and flipped through them as I went about the shopping.

With those rolls, however, I stopped to pick them up early in the morning on my way to work, rushed out of the store, drove to the office, parked, and waited until I was sitting at my desk before opening the envelope. I pulled out each picture slowly and scrutinized them one at a time. In one roll, Kat looked stunning. Not one picture showed her with her hand in her mouth or her eyes crossed. Pictures don't lie, I thought, overcome with a surge of hope.

I rushed to a friend who knew about, but had never met, Kat to show them to her.

"She's beautiful," she said, "and she looks completely normal and healthy."

"She does, doesn't she? She's going to be okay. She's really going to be okay," I said, totally believing it for a few hours.

Kat's constant companion had been a funny, handmade doll with curly brown yarn hair, a blue calico dress, and black painted eyes—a Raggedy Ann figure. I can't remember how it arrived or when Kat fell in love with it. One day it wasn't there. The next she clutched it to her like her life depended on it. She pulled its yarn hair, waved it in her outstretched arms, and hugged it to her chest. She kept it with her wherever she went, cried for it when it dropped, slept with it in her crib, brought it along for rides in the backpack. It was soft and supple with blue cloth shoes, white stockinged legs, and a perpetual smile.

The blue doll fit wherever Kat stuffed her and seemed happy as her curls loosened and her dress tore. Somehow, she seemed to love being with Katherine as much as Kat loved her.

I delighted in Kat's first attachment, pleased with her good taste and happy to see the look in her eye when she twirled the blue doll above her head and, giggling, brought it to her lap.

In our move, the blue doll disappeared. It didn't matter. Somewhere along the way Kat had stopped caring about it.

During this time, I began playing silly games with myself: If Chapel Hill makes it to the Final Four, Katherine will get better; if my dad's failing business turns around, that will be the sign of Katherine's recovery; if Paul wins his big case; if I make it to the grocery store and find a parking spot in four minutes; if I run all the way to Monaco Street and back without having to stop for traffic at Colorado Boulevard. Every day I created elaborate schemes, believing if I executed them flawlessly, if the fates favored me on these little things, then Katherine would get well.

In April of 1981 Paul's law firm held a retreat at a mountain resort. Paul Sr. and Rita took care of Katherine. Paul was in meetings all day. I strolled while he worked.

On a walk around the lake, I looked in a shop window and stopped stunned. There was Kat's blue doll, sitting on a wooden chest, smiling knowingly at me. It was as if a dear friend who had died appeared on my doorstep full of life. I stared at it for a long time, went in, paid the resort-area premium, and waited while the clerk wrapped it in pink tissue paper and put it in a hot-pink bag.

Somehow I thought if Kat could once again love her blue doll, she might also be able to love me, or show me that she loved me. I feared she had lost the capacity to love and that realization ripped my heart to shreds. I made another bet with myself: If Kat recognized the blue doll, it would be the turning point.

Paul Sr. and Rita brought Kat to meet us on Sunday. In the lobby, Kat looked tired and showed little interest as I hugged her to me. "She was a little angel," Rita said. "She ate well and was no trouble at all."

"Did her eyes cross?" I asked, always my first question.

"A little, but she followed my face real well and smiled a lot," Rita responded, too deeply in love with Katherine to tell the truth.

I had dreaded the reunion since I'd arrived at the retreat, unable to shake images of Katherine's greetings ten months before, when she always screeched with delight and reached her arms up to me with a big grin on her face. I didn't want to believe the child I had adored more than life itself cared so little for me now. Kat slumped on my lap and started wringing her hands. I hesitated before I reached deep in the pink bag—not sure I could handle one more defeat. Those little routs brought my greatest agony. They chipped away at the dream, slapping me across the face like a wet rag, leaving me with a sour smell, and showing me how little of my perfect Katherine was left.

I pulled out the blue doll and held it toward Kat. When she saw it, she squealed with delight, reached out, and grabbed it to her. It awakened something in her. She remembered.

Seconds later, the blue doll dropped to the floor and Kat paid no more attention to it.

On the drive home, Paul said, "Sue, I remember when I was a little boy, I'd see retarded people and think the worst thing that could happen in life was to grow up, get married, and have a retarded child. Now, it's like I'm being taught a lesson for those thoughts."

APRIL 15, 1981, JOURNAL ENTRY
Another cold, more eye crossing, acting crazy. Why not admit she is a dimwit, a retarded thing? She under-

stands so little. Why not admit there is no hope? Why not face reality? She will be our lifelong burden and sorrow. She is little more than a vegetable. Why has my precious child been turned into a drooling idiot? Why can no one help me when I keep begging for help?

I babysat for two children Katherine's age. I regretted it after I said I would. It was a day off. I had nothing planned. No one in the babysitting co-op had called for months. I thought everyone knew the worst thing for me was seeing what other children were able to do. The call caught me off guard. I said yes before I had time to think.

Katherine sat in the same spot on the floor wringing her hands and crossing her eyes as the children pirouetted around her, playing with every toy—including Kat's new blue doll—and exploring the house. Outside, they climbed on the jungle gym and played in the sandbox. I set Katherine on the brightly colored quilt my dad's mother had given Katherine as a baby present. Kat didn't move. She paid no attention to the other children. Since that brief moment after the retreat she'd shown no interest in the blue doll. She ignored the other toys I placed near her.

When the children's mothers picked them up, I told them Kat was napping and pretended all had gone well. After they left, I stuffed all the toys—except the blue doll—in a garbage bag, carried it to the alley behind our house, and threw it in the Dumpster. I put Katherine in the downstairs crib, went upstairs, and lay on my bed. I closed my eyes tight and tried to tell myself everything would be all right, but no words came.

Other mothers called, but I always made up excuses not to take care of their children. I stopped using the co-op. I couldn't stand having other people know how far gone Katherine was. Beneath my façade of competence, I was a mess. Where would I find the strength and patience to care for Kat? How could I cope with the added stress of a new baby? If I couldn't protect Katherine, how could I protect her sister or brother?

When sorrow has seeped into us, we will do anything to push it away, anything. We undertake our own Labors of Hercules.

During this time Paul had no energy and couldn't shake colds. We thought he might have mono, but his test results came back negative. He worked harder at Holland & Hart, never missed a day of work, and held everything inside. For months the fatigue stayed with him. He lost weight. It was as if he were wilting from a broken heart.

Night after night, Paul and I held onto each other, wrapping our arms and legs together, our skin merging as we tried to weave the tapestry of our lives, but unraveling went on all about us.

I began to do everything in my power to fix our broken child. We increased the speech, physical, and occupational therapy. I enrolled Kat in a preschool for developmentally delayed children. Nothing worked. We grew increasingly desperate, willing to try more and more far-out cures, willing to do anything to get Katherine back.

We took her to a macrobiotic clinic in Boulder. The man who saw her thought her respiratory and intestinal systems were "clogged up" and that improper diet was causing most of her problems. The macrobiotic diet he put us on consisted of grains, vegetables, fruits, fish, soy products, nuts, and miso—no milk products, meats, poultry, or bread. We studied books on nutrition to make sure she would get all the vitamins and minerals she needed, then began the diet with a vengeance. Paul and I smuggled ice cream and cookies on the side but kept Kat's diet absolutely pure for more than six months.

We called a Spanish *curandera*, an herb healer, who told us to put a garlic clove up Katherine's behind for ten days. If we saw change, she'd be able to help us. Katherine didn't change, but her room smelled like a cheap Italian restaurant for a week.

On a brief trip to Taos, we went to the Sanctuario de Chimayo, a New Mexican Lourdes. In the small dark room to the left of the chapel, we set Kat next to the dirt hole in the floor and rubbed the holy dirt on her body. Maybe we, too, would be able to tack a letter to the wall—

next to the crutches and photographs—telling of Katherine's miraculous recovery.

One Saturday when Paul was working, I took Katherine to a faith healer in Pueblo, a town two hours south of Denver. It was 100 degrees Fahrenheit. We baked in our Volvo station wagon, whose air conditioner had died. I opened the windows, creating a dry breeze that whistled through the car. The record-breaking July heat gave me a headache and ringlets of sweat-soaked hair around my face. Kat slept as I moved her from her car seat to her stroller and pushed her through the maze of cars in the huge lot.

A little man barked at the crowd from a small stage in the middle of the arena. Hordes of people circled 360 degrees around his protected island. Security men stood at the staircases to make sure energetic believers didn't rush up to be touched out of turn. When he finally finished his sermon, we pushed into the line. Slowly we made our way to the stage. I carried Katherine up the steps in her stroller. He looked at my large, pregnant belly and then at Kat.

"Don't you see all the people who need my healing?" he asked. "I'm not here to help the normal or unborn."

Quickly I explained. As quickly, he put his hands on Katherine's small shoulders and hurried us on.

Behind us in line was a slender woman with an aristocratic face and thick blond hair pulled back with a black lacquer barrette. She caught up with us after her turn and knelt down to talk to Katherine. She had received a similar reception until she told the "healer" she was dying of leukemia.

That was the Rainbow Grocery summer. After Katherine's morning therapy sessions, we'd often head to Rainbow, a store frequented by all the health-food addicts in the Denver area. The produce was organically grown. Bins of grains and beans lined the walls. I could buy seaweed in cellophane packages, and tofu was as common as cheese.

When I told the folks at the checkout Kat was on a macrobiotic diet, they nodded their heads in approval and began their stories: "I knew a guy once who was dying of cancer; macrobiotics cured him." "My sister never had any energy. Once she started a macrobiotic diet it was as if she were a new person." I'd go home and start boiling seaweed.

My immense belly began to tighten at Kat's therapy session on September 22, 1981. Katherine held the handles of a heavy wooden walking cart as the therapist moved her stiff legs, step-by-step. Mother sat by me on a metal folding chair in the large therapy room. She had arrived the day before to help with the new baby.

After the session we hurried home to fit in a walk while the morning air was fresh and cool. "How are you doing, Sue?" Mother kept asking. For a half hour, I assured her I was doing fine. Each time she asked, though,

I thought, God, how am I going to handle all of this—Kat, the new baby, work?

After a few shooting pains through my groin, the walking got tough. "Let's head home," I said. "Maybe something really is happening."

By the time we got back to the house, the contractions were coming every five minutes. I called Paul and asked him to meet us at the hospital.

The doctor checked me. "You're dilated to five centimeters. It's not a false alarm, but you have a few more hours."

An hour later, the contractions had grown intense. The doctor was nowhere to be found. Paul was calmer this time than he had been with Kat and more able to help. I lay on my side as he rubbed the small of my back and held my shoulders through severe contractions. When I felt the urge to push, I lost control.

"Find the doctor," I screamed to the nurse. "This baby is coming out." My yells turned to curses as the pain increased and it looked as if Paul was going to deliver the baby.

The doctor stepped sheepishly into the room. After one look, he quickly donned his surgical gloves. Several painful pushes later, Helen startled me with her first cry. There hadn't even been time to get to a delivery room.

I cuddled her against my chest and she began nursing. She was, as Katherine had been, remarkably beautiful and perfect. I felt an immediate bond and deep love. As I nursed

Helen—named for Paul's grandmother and the mythic Helen of Troy—pictures of Katherine before her illness floated to my mind. Much that I'd tried to block from my thoughts came washing over me. I felt incredible joy tinged with the sadness of knowing I could never feel safe to dream for Helen as I had with Katherine. I shelved the mental chart of Helen's future somewhere deep in my mind. I couldn't allow those hopes and aspirations. If I didn't dream, then the dreams couldn't be destroyed.

CHAPTER 5

PHOTO BY PAUL PHILLIPS

Helen, 6 months, 1982.

I had a conversation with a man who'd climbed Mount Everest. He asked me about my children. I told him about Katherine. "She's my Everest," I said. "No," he said, "Everest is easy in comparison. I had a choice to climb it. You didn't." At some point in our lives, each of us has a mountain, a huge looming mountain that we will have to climb. If we have the courage and strength to go forward step-by-step, valley-by-valley, ridge-by-ridge, little-by-little, we will make it to the top and find it looks different from anything we'd ever expected.

For every small gain Kat made, there were greater losses. The occupational, physical, and speech therapies were treadmills to nowhere. The preschool for developmentally delayed children couldn't break through to her. The macrobiotic diet gave her diarrhea, nothing more. The powers of the faith healer, the *curandera*, and the Chimayo holy dirt had no effect. We didn't know where to turn.

Then, on a stroll down Seventh Avenue in January 1982, I ran into a neighbor who knew Kat. She asked if I'd heard of something called "patterning." She told me of a brain-injured child she'd patterned in Michigan years before. "It was incredibly intense—loads of volunteers and a huge effort for the family—but I saw real progress."

"Could you find me the phone number? I'd love more information." Within a few hours, I'd called the Institutes for the Achievement of Human Potential, the home of patterning, located in Chestnut Hill near Philadelphia.

The Institutes' packet came on a bad day. At preschool Katherine had been lethargic and Helen had cried nonstop. I didn't know how I could go on balancing three days of work, the battery of therapy programs, and a small baby. When both girls were fed and down for naps, I pulled out the envelope with the fear that patterning would be one more dead end.

As I read, a profound sense of relief swept over me. Patterning wasn't a piecemeal approach—an hour here, an hour there. It was total immersion: a monumental effort—dawn to dark, with a hundred volunteers coming each week. Could it be we'd finally found the answer after everything we'd tried?

Glenn Doman, the founder of the Institutes, had developed patterning in the 1950s. It rested on the theory that by repetitiously imprinting the developmental stages of a normal child on the brain of an injured child, the brain could literally repair itself. The brain could be "repatterned" to normality by moving the limbs—millions of times—through the motions of crawling, creeping, and walking. The job of the volunteers was to physically move the child's limbs through those motions until the brain was programmed to act on its own. The earlier the program was started, the greater the chance for success because the brain was still developing.

Katherine had time on her side. She wasn't even two and a half. Patterning might be just what we needed to put Katherine's life back on track.

That evening I shared the materials with Paul. He read them carefully. When he looked up, the sadness that had been in his eyes for months had disappeared. "Sue, this just might be the answer. It rings true: the idea of retraining the brain by tapping into all those extra brain cells most of us never use."

"What've we got to lose?" I asked. "And think of what we might gain."

"It gives me new hope, Sue. We can do it."

⤛

We search. We move along straight paths and come upon detours that take us to the most unexpected places. We keep going. Sometimes all that matters is that we are moving someplace. It doesn't matter where.

I quit my job and walked door-to-door in the neighborhood to recruit volunteers. We needed one hundred people, each to come for an hour-and-a-half session once a week. We prepared a letter with a picture of Kat on the top asking for help. With Helen in a backpack and Katherine in a stroller, I knocked on doors of people I'd never met.

My mouth was dry with apprehension as I knocked on those doors—the same feeling I'd experienced selling books door-to-door in Columbia, South Carolina, one summer during college—never knowing what awaited after the knock. At the Southwestern Company, we were taught all sorts of tricks, including literally getting a foot in the door—or at least part of your body so the door couldn't be closed—discreet, but bold. I learned every technique for success: smiling, setting people at ease, focusing on their children's education. Most of all, every time I knocked on a door, I believed I'd sell a book. My cousin Blair, who sold with me that summer, had just the opposite view. He couldn't believe his good fortune when he made a sale. He celebrated with a milk shake at Burger King. One sale made his day. At the end of the day, he measured his success by the number of free meals, glasses of iced tea, or bowls of ice cream he'd been given by bighearted housewives. I sold more books. Blair had more fun.

That summer I won an award as one of the top five salespeople out of two thousand college kids. I didn't know I was practicing for the most important sales job of my life. No one closed the door on me with Helen on my back and Katherine in the stroller. When I went in to sell them on Kat and the need to save her, it was the best sales pitch of my life. I had never believed in anything more.

Many neighbors signed up and became dear friends. A sign at our local elementary school attracted six of my best volunteers. More than twenty people from Paul's law firm—secretaries to senior partners—joined us. Several people heard about Kat from a friend of a friend. Paul's dad drove two hours from Winter Park every Thursday morning.

It took a month to attract all the volunteers and build up to a full program. Once there, we worked with Kat fourteen hours a day, 365 days a year—Christmas, Easter, Thanksgiving—for three years.

Much later I realized I had prepared for patterning as a child. When I was eleven, living in Woodsfield, Ohio, Dad came home and told us we were going to build a tennis court. "It'll be a good family project," he said. "We'll finish it this summer."

The backhoe came and flattened the backyard. Loads of dirt were delivered and piled in giant red pyramids. The workers left. We began. I spent most of my eleventh summer sifting dirt and stomping clay. We shoveled dirt hour after hour until it was as fine as flour. We carted the precious loads to the section of the court then under construction. We worked methodically, step-by-step. By July, half the court was finished. The red clay lay smooth and firm. We started in on the second side, sifting until we had blisters on our hands and a sense of accomplishment as sweet as any I've ever tasted. Dad taught us that pure, blind persistence was all it would take to transform the yard—or our life—into whatever we wanted it to be.

Dad grew up a short, smart kid in a small town in North Dakota. He skipped a grade in high school, graduated as valedictorian, then went on to West Point, and fought in the Korean War. He never bailed us out if we were in trouble. He wouldn't have known how. With his never saying a word, we knew if you made a mistake, you paid for it; if you worked hard, you reaped the rewards.

I don't remember my father reading to me or tucking me into bed. I don't remember hugs or affectionate words. I remember him working with me on long Saturday afternoons unraveling the mysteries of chemistry. I remember him rushing home from work to take us skiing at the rope tow twenty miles away.

Dad spent hours throwing tennis balls to us that summer. What he lacked in technique, he made up for in doggedness. He stood behind us and held our right arms, taking us through the motions of a swing. He threw balls that we hit over the fence and up the sloping hill. He never complained. He kept throwing and throwing until finally we learned the game.

Dad never let me off the hook because I was a girl. He didn't advise me to skip science or math. He insisted on As there. He encouraged me to go to Yale Law School. When I wanted to go to France to live with a family, sell books door-to-door, or drive cross-country, he never said no. He didn't say much, in fact.

In his midfifties, he was let go from Olin Corporation after twenty-five years in management positions. Rather than take it easy and retire on his nest egg, he sank his life's savings into a struggling company in New Haven that produced telephone coil cords. High interest rates and outmoded equipment doomed his company. A couple of years after Kat started her downward spiral, Dad declared bankruptcy. We hit bottom together, neither of us able to help the other. One of the company's plants in New Hampshire survived the bankruptcy. Dad went on to run it. Like a North Dakota farmer, he is a survivor, taking life's storms, droughts, and spring rains as they come.

Dad never fed Kat, dressed her, or carried her to her room to snuggle with her. We never discussed Katherine. He never asked how I was doing or what it was like. Somehow, all through my life I had believed he'd be there for me if ever I really needed him.

With Kat, he wasn't there. But he had taught me all about hard work, resilience, and doing what needed to be done, even if it was impossible. It never occurred to me that I couldn't put together a top-notch volunteer corps. This was the most important work I'd ever do. I was saving Katherine's life. Nothing would stand in my way.

Sometimes we are deserted by those we've trusted most. "It's your problem," they say, perhaps not even realizing they've turned away, unable to reach out a hand. When we've been abandoned, we go deep within and, over time, find our strength. We go far outside and, over time, find teachers in unexpected friends.

We couldn't wait. We found a man from Atlanta who traveled the country setting up patterning programs for families and flew him out to get us started. We began patterning on March 1, 1982.

MAY 25, 1982, JOURNAL ENTRY
Our eighth wedding anniversary and a banner day. Katherine went across the laundry room floor on her belly by herself twice today. She also grabbed for a

spoon with her left hand and put it in her mouth. Already she's doing so well and when we get to the Institutes for the Achievement of Human Potential, I know it will be even better. Someday I hope I will be able to tell Katherine's story and do it justice—the story of a little girl's fight to touch life.

JUNE 8, 1982, JOURNAL ENTRY

I want the energy to write or read or do something productive, but it is gone. I can hardly move. I am nauseated with worry and fear. Death appeals to me like water in a desert. It seems the only thing that can remove the constant ache. We should give up the whole program and put Katherine away somewhere where she will sit in a corner all day, rubbing her hands, smacking her lips. She would be happy, but I never would be unless I resigned myself to the belief there was nothing begging to be let out behind those eyes that—at times—shine so brightly.

Bathe Helen, bathe Katherine, feed Helen, feed Katherine, dress Helen, dress Katherine, fix breakfast, lunch, and dinner, pattern, get Katherine to creep, to crawl. Paul helped when he was home, but his work took much of his time. Patterning was his second job. It was my first and took every ounce of energy I had. I felt jealous as he left the house each day, but I wouldn't have traded places. Only I, the supermom, could do what needed to be done, only I could make it happen.

Volunteers called to cancel. Each time the phone rang,

my heart dropped. I made tons of calls for substitutes, saying little prayers before dialing their numbers. When I struck out, I filled in and did all four daily sessions, while trying to keep Helen entertained.

By the end of the day, after all of Katherine's sessions, when finally both children were fed, changed, and asleep, I crawled into bed, numb.

CHAPTER 6

PHOTO BY PAUL PHILLIPS

Katherine, age 4, 1983.

We break. We wonder whether it is worth going on. We want to escape all the feelings. We grow numb and stay numb—sometimes for a short time, sometimes for a long time. Finally, an awakening begins. We smell a flower, see a beautiful painting, feel the wind on our faces. We blow bubbles, fly a kite, run through a field under a full moon. We feel again, and we are stronger in the broken places.

WE PULLED into the Pike Motel at midnight the night before our first visit to the Institutes for the Achievement of Human Potential. We were exhausted from the plane trip and the drive from New Haven where we'd left Helen with my parents, but also filled with the hope that this was Kat's—and our—only chance for a normal life. That August week in Chestnut Hill, it rained every day and there was a continual chill in the air.

A strong urine smell rose from the carpet. There were no washcloths, one tiny bar of soap, and two thin towels the size of large handkerchiefs. After changing Kat, putting her into a blanket sleeper, and nestling her in the wooden fold-up crib, Paul and I dropped into bed, sinking to the middle of the lumpy mattress. The couple in the next room argued the night away as trucks rushed by on the highway, rattling the windows. The next day we moved to the nearby Sheraton, twice as expensive but clean.

Paul was doing well at Holland & Hart, but partnership was a couple of years away. With the new house, two children, the shift to one income, the expense of the trips to Chestnut Hill, and the cost of the Institutes' program (nearly $400 a month), we had nothing to spare. But giving Kat a chance was worth everything to us.

People jammed the Institutes' gymnasium that first morning. Children lay on the floor barely able to move.

Others ran around in a hyperactive stupor. A thirty-year-old accident victim lay comatose on a stretcher, his mother wiping his head with a cloth.

They were all shapes and sizes. They were hurt, powerless, dispossessed, cast-off. They had been whole once, but life had taken a turn. Through accident, fever, lack of oxygen, trauma, their lives were forever changed.

One beautiful little girl, a couple of years older than Kat, stood clasping her hands and walking with a stiff-legged gait, looking nowhere. I couldn't take my eyes off her. She reminded me so much of Katherine. Later, I learned she, too, had received a diagnosis of viral encephalitis.

Few of the parents made eye contact. They looked earnest and frightened. I tried to tell myself we were different, that Katherine didn't really fit in. But I knew we were all there for the same reason. That morning in the Institutes' gymnasium changed me forever. For the first time, sitting in the midst of the chaos, I realized how completely Katherine belonged to the world of the brain injured.

We waited several hours until Katherine's name was called. We followed a leathery-faced, gruff-voiced Australian woman, who was to serve as Katherine's "advocate," through a maze of people to examining rooms where detailed baseline data were gathered—Kat's weight, height, chest measurement, head circumference—and an array of tests was performed to try to determine her level of cognitive understanding.

It was after 9:00 PM when we left the gymnasium. We stopped to eat on the way back to the hotel. I felt leaden, unable to speak. Moving my arms and legs took total concentration. Paul spooned ice cream into Kat's mouth as I held her. When she drifted to sleep, I rested my head against hers and wondered how the emptiness that permeated every fiber of my being would ever be filled.

On a visit to the Denver Zoo, I saw a deformed child being carried along a path. She smiled and laughed, yet her body was twisted and tormented. Before, I'd looked at the handicapped with a cold sympathy. No longer. Their plight had become my plight. We were forever connected.

"Congratulations; you have a brain-injured child," Glenn Doman boomed at the start of the second morning. Over the next few days he told gripping stories of what it meant to be brain injured. The brain began fine. Along the way disease or trauma changed its course. We the parents, with total dedication and superhuman effort, had it within our power to set the course straight once more. By the time Doman completed his lectures congratulating us on our fate, we believed him. He captured us in his web of oratory. We felt privileged and believed our chance for heroism lay in our ability to fix our children.

Doman spoke with passion about the potential within each of them. He told a World War II story that ended with the phrase "you never leave the wounded behind." Our children were like brave warriors shattered by bullets. We couldn't leave them to die on the battlefield when they could be saved. He told another story of a boy whose younger brother had been severely hurt. As the younger boy grew heavier, people asked the older brother how he could continue to carry him day after day. "He's not heavy, he's my brother" was his response.

He told of climbing mountains in Iran. The first day out, his party toiled from one range to another in a heavy mist. At dusk, he looked ahead discouraged with what little progress they'd made. When he looked back, he was startled when he saw how far they'd come. He spoke of struggles and triumphs, but mainly of the power within us to fix our kids.

Early that week, we were handed the Doman-Delacato Developmental Profile, an intricate chart that outlined seven stages of brain development, starting from the most basic at birth to the most sophisticated at about age six. It included sections on mobility, language, and manual, visual, tactile, and auditory competence: the stages our children would progress through. A depression came over me. It all seemed too neat, too planned. Katherine's strange behavior didn't fit on a chart. I couldn't shake the sinking feeling.

The fact is we were desperate. It was impossible to substantiate any of the claims of success made by the Institutes. But the Institutes was our last chance and we knew that all too well. Everything else had failed. We had no other options. We would have done anything to make Kat normal. And if we couldn't make her normal, we had no idea how we could cope or if we could cope.

During Doman's lectures, Paul asked several probing questions about the Developmental Profile and how the brain's excess capacity could be put to use. After one session, Paul went up to Doman to talk. Doman, who by then did no direct work with the children, said he'd like to see our child. We felt like we'd been touched by a god.

The next morning, my thirty-first birthday, we took Kat to him. I dressed her in a smocked dress with a matching bonnet. Kat mouthed her hands, dropped her head, and showed no response to Doman's efforts to engage her. Doman watched her closely and then said, gently, words that sank into our spirits like ice: "Children like Katherine scare me."

SEPTEMBER 1, 1982, JOURNAL ENTRY
Our first visit to the Institutes is behind us. My feelings are mixed. I know they will do everything they can to help Katherine. Yet I have nagging doubts they won't be able to crack her shell.

As we took off, I wished this plane would go down, taking Katherine and me out of this world, leaving

Paul and Helen free [Paul and Helen had flown home earlier], ending my pain, removing forever the hate and tension I feel toward Katherine. As she sleeps next to me, her little hands at peace, her mouth puckered, I can hardly believe the hell I live with. Yet I see that sleeping child as an angel.

Back in Denver, we resumed patterning with total dedication. On September 6, during the morning session, Katherine began crawling back and forth on the concrete floor in our laundry room.

I called Paul. "She's crawling. She's crawling!" I said, picturing him at his desk piled high with files.

"You're kidding," he said.

"No, she's really doing it great. Something clicked."

"Yes!" he yelled, and I imagined him raising his fist to the sky. "That little rascal is going to get herself well."

Within a week, Katherine crawled nearly a quarter of a mile a day. By mid-September she had already reached her November Institutes' goal. Yet, when left alone, she never crawled to get anywhere.

I needed help. A couple of months into the Institutes' program, we began renovating our garage into a small apartment. We found a woman, Mary, who moved in. She ran one of the sessions each day and helped care for Helen. A heavyset, bighearted woman, Mary embraced Kat and Helen and brought a lighthearted playfulness to the house.

During this time, Helen brightened our lives like a rainbow in a storm-darkened sky. At a year, she was walking, talking, and climbing up and down stairs. We adored her, but felt an even greater loss when we knew how easily things came to her. With Kat we hadn't experienced the miracle of normal development, the effortlessness of achieving milestones, the natural, beautiful progression. With Helen, it all seemed so simple. She was a little elf running literal and figurative circles around her sister, showing us just how far Katherine really had to go.

Each morning it seemed like an offering to the gods as the volunteers surrounded Katherine in our basement with its tiny windows and gray barn-siding walls. The volunteers chanted nursery rhymes and sang songs as they moved Kat's body through the patterns. Kat smiled, stiffened a leg to break the pattern, laughed, crawled for lollipops, forced her body to do the impossible to make their ceremony complete.

The Institutes' patterning program included work on all of Katherine's senses. To improve her vision, a strobe light blinked on and off. We made and showed her thousands of word cards to teach her to read. We brushed her hands and feet with scrub brushes to awaken her sense of feel. A handyman friend built a noise box to break through to her hearing. The unassuming box roared a sound somewhere between a fire drill and an ambulance siren. The first time we tried it, Kat nearly jumped off the patterning table. Later, she tensed and squinted, trying to figure out what was going on.

Katherine's altar was the patterning table, a rectangular structure the height of a kitchen counter. Paul had built it, covering it with foam and brown Naugahyde, cutting out a semicircle for her head. We began each session with Kat sitting at the end of the patterning table as the noise box blasted on and off for five minutes. Then came the heart of the program. Kat lay on her stomach for ten minutes of patterning: One patterner moved her head from side to side, one controlled her feet, and one was at each of her sides. They moved her small body to a rhythmic beat: On one side, as her arm went up, her leg went down; then her arm came down and her leg bent up. The other side did the same movement in the opposite pattern. The person at the end held her feet, moving them up and down, bringing control and symmetry.

The volunteers sang to maintain the rhythm of the pattern. "This Old Man," "Mary Had a Little Lamb," "My Country 'Tis of Thee" rang up from the basement for four hour-and-a-half sessions a day.

At times, Kat's joy shone through. Her eyes twinkled. The imp in her found a voice. At other times, she lay exhausted, worn down by the outpouring of attention, tired out by the demands of a program committed to regrowing her body and brain. She got sick. We pushed her to go on. She was so far behind and we were so desperate for her to catch up.

Our neighbors who weren't patterning must have thought we were running a drug ring. The same people returned each week for their fix. The noise box, the flashing lights, the cheering, the songs—all these strange rituals were for Katherine.

Many nights Paul left me. He went to the guest room in another wing of the house, two staircases away from me and the children. He'd start out beside me but wake in the middle of the night and leave in the darkness. We went through the motions: getting up, playing with Helen, patterning, going to work, eating dinner. We were together, but apart.

I loved him, but I didn't talk to him. We talked around each other. We couldn't have the conversation we needed. Neither of us had the courage to break into the nugget of pain and let it out. If we talked about our fears, our realization of Katherine's limits, our despair and darkness, it might somehow prevent Kat from getting better. Perhaps we both knew we were on an impossible quest. I blamed Paul for that drink of water, yet we didn't really know if it had caused Kat's condition. We knew so little about what had happened to our once-perfect child. We were like rats in a maze, going round and round, doing what we were programmed to do. We didn't want to stop.

We couldn't. The mindlessness of the effort kept us from confronting a reality that was too bleak for us to handle.

In the mornings before the patterners came, Paul and I spent two hours showing Kat word cards and getting her to crawl. We worked day in, day out, but we never felt further apart. I thrust myself headlong into patterning. Paul immersed himself in work, climbing the ladder at his law firm. He helped with patterning. He showed Kat the word cards, filled in for evening sessions, acted the gracious host for the patterners, went with me for the weeklong visits to the Institutes. He, too, would have done anything for Kat. But he left the house each day. He could direct his mind to other things. I could not.

When Paul found me crying, a grimace of pain crossed his face. I couldn't look his way. Everything in him had crumpled. He built dikes around his heart to keep the pain in its place. When he saw me, the water started leaking out and it was as if his very being would fall apart.

I began to hide my tears from him, wiping the lines from my cheeks and washing the red out of my eyes before he got home from work. He'd complain about being tired. I'd think of my day and have no sympathy.

The patterners were a phenomenal support system, but I couldn't let them see my fears. Though I was surrounded by people, I retreated into myself, growing further from Paul. For years the chasm grew. I went my way and he went his. It was as if each of us was wrapped in a cocoon of our own making, unable to break out to soothe the other.

Paul once said, "Sue, I was raised with the West Point motto, 'Duty, Honor, Country.' I'll always stand by Katherine." My father, like Paul's a West Point graduate, had instilled a similar sense of duty in me. The routine of duty created a veneer that kept us going but hid the loneliness beneath it.

I ran often. I sweated and felt my muscles working. Usually, by the time I'd jogged around Cheesman Park or out Seventh Avenue to Monaco, the tension was gone and I could return to the constant action in our house. When the weather was bad and I missed a day of running, the tension built.

One night Paul came home and handed me three jump ropes. "Try this," Paul suggested. "It's great exercise and you can do it on the days you can't fit in a run. I wasn't sure which type you'd like best."

I chose my favorite rope and developed an elaborate routine: five hundred jumps fast on both feet; five hundred jumps alternating left foot, right foot; five hundred jumps slower with a small skip in between; and five hundred jumps fast again with both feet. It was one of the best gifts I'd ever received. When I couldn't run, I'd jump until my calves hurt. I'd think of the effort it took for Katherine to crawl back and forth on the laundry room floor and I'd feel closer to her.

⤳

Nothing is going right. No one is able to help. Those we thought would be there for us are nowhere to be found. Those we most love can't reach out to us. "Why me?" repeats in our brains as our anger and frustration grows—at our spouses, our friends, our relatives, everyone. We cry. We scream. No one hears us. We keep moving and somewhere far down the path, the "Why me?" turns into "Yes, me."

Kat was chubby then, with soft cheeks and pudgy hands. Between patterning sessions, I'd sit in the basement showing her word cards, large white cards with single words in bold red. The goal of the word cards—part of the Institutes' "intelligence program"—was to teach the children to read.

Sometimes Katherine looked at each one. Other times, she'd look everywhere but at the cards. At first when she looked away, I'd talk to her. When she kept doing it, I'd hold her head so it was easier. When even then she didn't look, I'd pinch those glorious cheeks. I'd shake her. I wanted to awaken her. My whole body tensed with anger when she wouldn't look. I'd retreat to my bedroom and try to get away, but I couldn't find a quiet spot where Kat wasn't on my mind.

When she didn't look at the word cards, I thought she was defying me. I was working so hard for her and she gave so little in return. I lost sight of the reality of her life. She may have had to look at the cards sideways in order to see. At those moments I saw the futility of the gigantic effort. I hated my life. I was a Yale-trained lawyer and I spent my days in our basement, showing Kat word cards, enticing her to crawl, and running patterning sessions. I wanted out but didn't know how to get out. Kat, through her indifference, showed me it didn't work, couldn't work. I didn't want to hear that. Kat and I had a pact. Against all odds, we were going to overcome. No matter what anyone said, together we could fix her. I couldn't stand it when she herself showed me how ridiculous my dream was.

The weeklong visits to the Institutes, at first every three months and then every six, became our vacations. We had neither the time nor the money for anything else. During our second trip in December 1982, Paul and I took long walks through Chestnut Hill's drizzle. At every opportunity we escaped the Institutes' rolling, tree-covered grounds. We went to the part of Chestnut Hill where people led normal lives.

Away from our basement's red shag carpet, the volunteers, and the noise box, we could pretend. We wrapped Kat in a pink poncho with a small hood and pushed her before us. I looked at the stone houses with attached greenhouses, regal gardens, and maids' quarters and imagined I was matriarch of the estate, living a perfect life in a perfect house in a perfect town with perfect children and a perfect husband.

We strolled down one street after another admiring the grand copper beeches, elms, and oaks. I switched from one favorite house to another. Many would do. I imagined the life and saw myself at its center—a carefree life bordered by the causes I carefully chose, not those that chose me.

Then Kat would scream a monotone screech and the falseness of my fantasy dawned on me. It crumbled around me. The rain came harder. I was left standing on a street corner in one of the most elegant places in America with a chill in my heart and a wish that I were anywhere in the world but Chestnut Hill.

I dreamed I was back at Chapel Hill in a classroom with wooden seats and desks. I held Katherine in my arms. She was listless, very hurt, very retarded. There was no question about the extent of her problem. But the class went on around us, not aware of Katherine. All I could do was hold her and try to do my work. In another dream, I was at a picnic with Tom, my first boyfriend; his wife; and their healthy children. Katherine lay beside me on a blanket, unable to move. The morning after those dreams, I woke aching, hardly able to pull myself from the bed, my day clouded, frightened by the messages from my unconscious.

MAY 12, 1983, JOURNAL ENTRY

My dearest Paul,

I know I will not give this to you, but I have to write
it. We must face the truth. Katherine is not getting
better. She is getting worse. There is nothing more we
can do to help her. I cannot continue living the way I
have for the past fifteen months. The constant tension
and pressure for so little are more than I can take.

Kat could once stand—no more. She could once
pick up food with her fingers and put it in her
mouth—no more. She could once take a spoon with
her left hand and put it in her mouth—no more. She
once said several words a day—no more. She has lost
more than she has gained.

The colds literally may never go away. They may be
symptoms just like the hand-wringing. More and more,
I believe we are fools to remain blind to the reality.

I can't keep smiling for all of the people coming to
my house when I am growing to hate Kat for what she
has done to my life. You can't imagine how often I
want to leave it all behind and start anew, somewhere
far away by myself, with nothing to remind me of the
past three years.

I know you adore Kat—as do I—but I have given
up all hope of her ever being remotely normal. If I am to
go on living here, we must find a place for Katherine
where she can be loved and cared for. How can we keep
Katherine with us? The disappointment is too great. I

fear my bitterness about Kat, about the life I'm leading,
is like an abscess that will continue to grow, leaving an
infection that will never heal. I can take no more . . .

*We walk a taut but fragile tightrope. At any second a slight
wind might come along and knock us off, right to sanity, left
to madness. In our crises, we experience both fully.*

CHAPTER 7

Alice, Helen, and Katherine, summer 1984.

Pain digs deep into us. It gnaws, destroys, transforms. It throws all of life's intensity like mud at our faces and keeps us wallowing, stuck, frantic, not sure we can make our way out. It brings us to depths we never imagined and, because of that, allows us heights we never contemplated.

I FELT the familiar heaviness and tiredness, the faint stirring in the belly. When I went to the obstetrician, he merely confirmed my suspicions. I was pregnant again despite an IUD. When he removed it, there was a slight chance I would miscarry the baby. I didn't know what I wanted. Paul said little, but later told me, "I didn't know how we'd cope. We were already holding on by our fingernails. Another child would add more complexity to our already too complex lives. I had real feelings of dread, but knew at another level that it would be all right, that it would be good in the end."

Just after her fourth birthday, Katherine crawled a mile in one day. The volunteers cheered when she passed the red tape marker on the laundry room floor. They hugged each other. They hugged Katherine. Kat knew what she'd done. She grinned and giggled. Then, while the patterners were still exalting, she dropped to sleep in my arms. The next day, I wrote:

SEPTEMBER 7, 1983, JOURNAL ENTRY
So often I'm tired and start out angry that I have to do one more day of patterning. And yet Katherine, no matter how tired, does it day after day. She is a great champ regardless of the outcome of the program and her life. How I wish I could get inside her mind and see what goes on, what she understands, what brings

her pleasure. Maybe one of these days, she'll be able to tell us all those things.

I sit crying for so many reasons—both sad and happy. Yesterday Katherine crawled a mile. She met her November goal. She knew what she was doing. She wanted to do it. We pushed her on and she made it. Then, this morning, we started again relentlessly pushing her. Never stop. She goes on—that courageous child with such limitations.

I find myself with a kind of malaise—thrilled with what Kat has done, yet exhausted when I think of what still must be done. Katherine has not played with a toy for three years.

Later in September, Paul made partner at Holland & Hart. We popped the champagne on Wednesday night, the day he was told. Thursday, he came home with an announcement.

"Sue, we're going to San Francisco tomorrow morning. Pack your bags."

"But what about patterning, taking care of the kids this weekend?"

"Mary's on for us. She said she was happy to give you a break. We're set, girl. We need this."

We ate seafood sauté at Tadich's, walked the Marin Headlands early in the morning as the sun rose, stalked a blue heron in the Muir Woods, and felt again the depth of our love, which was so challenged by the reality of our lives. The trip was a refreshing, but momentary, escape. We had to return quickly to our real lives with Katherine.

When I was seven months pregnant, Mary and I took Katherine to Chestnut Hill. We'd patterned Katherine for nearly two years. I wanted Mary to know the new patterning program inside out so she could cover for me when the baby was born.

We hit a snowstorm on our drive down from New Haven where we'd dropped Helen with my parents. I saw it as a sign. Though it was our fourth trip to the Institutes, waiting in the chaotic gymnasium hadn't gotten any easier for me. I'd watch the children in Katherine's "class," looking for miracles of progress. Always I was disappointed. When I put Katherine down on the wooden floor hoping she'd show off her fine crawl, she didn't move.

Hours passed. Katherine fell asleep right before her name was called. She woke from her nap and perked up during the evaluation. I held up a group of two-word couplets—in bright red on twelve-inch squares of white cardboard—and asked, "Katherine, which is 'Bounce, please,' or 'Wave, Mommy,' or 'Hug Kat'?" Each time Katherine looked at the right one and smiled. She was given a "reading victory."

She'd grown an inch and a half taller. Her head circumference had grown twice as fast as normal, and her chest, from the hours and hours of crawling, had grown at a rate 267 percent of normal. The Institutes rated her progress "excellent" but said we had to make her progress faster. Her new program included crawling a mile and doing sixty trips across the overhead ladder each day; and an "intelligence program" that involved learning fractions and equations, reading books, and looking at more than a hundred different words a day.

By this time Katherine never voluntarily used her hands, though she could hang from a bar off the ground for ten minutes. She didn't feed herself or play with toys. She never pushed to a stand. She never crawled anywhere of her own accord. I knew the new program was beyond Kat's reach.

In that crowded gymnasium, I wondered—as I had many times before in the chilling quiet of my bedroom at night—if patterning was helping Kat or tormenting her; if we were heroes on a rescue mission or fools who couldn't accept reality.

On our last day, rain soaked Chestnut Hill, covering the fallen leaves with a slick film. Mary, Katherine, and I had sat in the crowded gymnasium for more than twelve hours to be taught the final pieces of the new program we'd implement on our return to Denver.

Rain beat down as we headed back to the motel. Midway down a long hill, the light changed. After a moment's hesitation, I stepped hard on the brakes. The car spun in the middle of the road, slipping on the slick leaves. Reflections from headlights blinded me. I couldn't tell if a car was coming behind us. Finally, we hit the median's concrete curb and came to an abrupt stop with a flat back tire.

As the car spun around, I somehow knew I'd never go back to the Institutes. We patterned for another fifteen months, but our visits to Chestnut Hill were over. We weren't getting anywhere; we were just spinning out of control.

Contractions began in the midst of our Friday evening patterning on January 27, 1984. Several hours later, I held Alice.

Alice—named for my grandmother's sister—looked like Katherine. She had Katherine's thick, black hair; delicate features; and huge eyes. There are baby pictures where we can't tell Kat and Alice apart.

Alice came out kicking and screaming and never stopped. Remembering the IUD, we called her our "kid who was meant to be." At a year, she weighed only seventeen pounds and walked upright under tables, making up for her small size with extra feistiness and daring. She was a little elf always into trouble, always on the go. Was this how Kat would have been?

In my dream, Alice is a small child. We are walking on a lake partially covered with ice. The ice breaks and Alice falls in. I find myself on the shore looking out at the dark lake, every muscle tense, not knowing where she is. I see several people in wet suits swimming across the lake. As soon as the first arrives at the shore, I plead to use his wet-suit top. I don't ask for his help. I don't explain my predicament. I quickly don the wet-suit top and swim frantically.

It's dark. During the swim, thousands of thoughts cross my mind. I realize that I've probably lost Alice. The chance of finding her in time is remote. I swim on and dive at the place I think Alice has gone down. The first thing I feel on the lake's floor is Alice. A sense of relief flows over me as I bring her to the surface, though the foreboding remains. She has been under a long time.

We're on the shore. Alice lies limp in my arms. The panic continues. Then her body begins to move. She opens her eyes and smiles. Alice I can save.

With patterning, we kept Katherine on her belly so she could crawl. To prevent her from sitting, we built an anti-sit device, a canvas vest with bent aluminum tubing sticking out that forced her down if she tried to sit up. She looked like an ungainly spider moving awkwardly around the sunroom floor. She outsmarted the device time and again. We redesigned it. She outsmarted it. It was a bizarre cat-and-mouse game. Ultimately she won. One day we took the antisit device off her forever. By then she couldn't stand alone. In our fervent efforts to get her to crawl, she'd lost all ability to stand. Even with the many thousands of hours devoted to patterning, we hadn't come close to creating a sequence of development that worked for her.

"It's not helping her, Paul," I said that overcast March day in 1985. Katherine had just turned five and a half. "It's been three years and she's made so little progress. She has so far to go. I don't think she can ever get where we want her to be."

We sat in the downstairs sunroom: the red tile floor cold as stone; the evening light fading; the grapevines choking the paned windows.

Paul sat next to me on the sofa holding my hand. The children slept. We were alone with the silence of Katherine's life.

For weeks I'd built my courage to talk to him about it. For a year I'd known, but I had been unable to admit it. The stress of maintaining the program with such minimal results had finally gotten too great.

Around the time Alice was born, I had dipped back into work. My former boss and I had started taking on legal projects and began an organization to improve public schools. I worked fifteen to twenty hours a week, squeezing it in on weekends and evenings. I relied more on the volunteers and our babysitter, Mary, telling myself I didn't need to be there for every patterning session. I knew I needed to find a life for myself beyond our basement. Even so, I couldn't imagine life without patterning.

When the end finally came, I held Paul's hand tightly, not wanting to ever let go, feeling that if I did I would fall apart. I had to hold on to something.

"We've done our best for Kat," he said. "We couldn't have done more."

"I don't know what I'll do with her when we stop. I don't know how I'll fill my hours with her. I don't know if I can give up on her, sit back and do nothing. It's like I can't live with her and I can't live without her. Maybe we need to find a home for her, but how can we be sure she'd get good care? How would we know how she was being treated?" When the tears came, I took my hand from his and covered my face, trying to hide the despair.

"It's okay, Sue. It's okay. We did all we could do," Paul said, putting an arm around me. Then he sat, silent. We knew it wasn't okay.

I left the room, walked through the narrow kitchen, and grabbed a sweater off the hook by the back door. I walked slowly down Seventh Avenue. I had always been afraid of walking alone in Denver at night. That night I didn't care what happened.

How could I tell the patterners who had been so loyal? How would I admit defeat? How would I manage with no driving routine to keep away my despair?

I walked past a Catholic church and sat on a brick wall. Tears no longer came. Now that we'd come to an end, I didn't know where to begin. There were no road maps for overcoming sorrow.

"God, I was worried," Paul said when I walked in an hour later. "Are you all right?"

"I'll be all right if you hold me and don't say a word. I just need time."

Over the next week, I told the patterners. Many didn't want to stop. They asked if they could still visit Katherine. "We'll miss her. She has meant so much to us."

I thought of the piece KCNC Channel 4 had done on Katherine the year before. The newscaster interviewed volunteers as they patterned. When asked why they kept coming back, Hillary Weed, an elderly widow, stopped the pattern, looked the newscaster directly in the eye, and said, "It's a two-way street, you know. Katherine gives as much as she gets."

Why do we dread endings, even when the endings make way for new beginnings?

CHAPTER 8

Katherine, Alice, Helen, and Mark, summer 1986.

If we can get through this, we can get through anything. Anything life throws us, we can withstand. We learn more from our trials than from our triumphs. What power our sorrow can give us.

BOETTCHER SCHOOL sat across the street from Children's Hospital. The week before we stopped patterning, we visited Boettcher, a public school for the handicapped. I parked in the same spot I had years before when I'd taken Katherine to early morning therapy at Children's. Then I had stood her proudly on the sidewalk, until one day she fell and cut her head on the car door. Three years later, she couldn't stand at all. I no longer had any illusions about our ability to fix her.

Helen and Alice ran beside me as I pushed Kat. Helen held Alice's hand, at three the big sister, trying to keep fourteen-month-old Alice headed in the right direction. Katherine's head drooped.

After being hit by the institutional smell and the sterile green walls, we found the office. The secretary pointed down the hallway to the classroom that would become Kat's.

Both teachers greeted Katherine warmly. They lifted her out of the stroller and put her on a pad on the floor where they sat next to her clapping her hands and talking to her with their faces close to hers. Katherine grinned and rocked back and forth. They explained that the daily routine included music, videos, gym, and art projects where they'd work on Katherine's sense of touch. Several children lay on mats unable to walk. Others moved haphazardly around the classroom.

I left, comfortable with the place and grateful to the

teachers but fully aware of what taking this step meant: The rest of Katherine's life would be spent among life's wounded. My attempt to make her life normal had failed.

The night before Katherine started at Boettcher, I lay in bed tossing and turning. Images of Katherine flashed through my mind over and over again. I pictured her at her birth; riding behind me in the bike seat; sitting in her stroller bringing a toe to her mouth. I heard her giggle as she hugged her blue doll; saw her drink the water from the mountain stream; then watched as, at fifteen months, she sat on Paul's shoulders in her velvet Christmas dress, one hand holding onto Paul's head, the other stuffed in her mouth as her eyes crossed. I remembered the high fevers and seizures and how we thought if we could just get her well, we could get her better.

I saw her crawling across the kitchen's linoleum floor in the antisit device, her jaw set in determination as she got near her peanut butter and jelly sandwich; lying on the patterning table sound asleep, exhausted from the day's work; walking haltingly to the end of the overhead ladder and bursting into a smile when the patterners cheered—a beautiful, brave child, just too hurt to ever have the normal life I so wanted for her. The images kept coming until I was left with nothing except a throbbing dread of the future.

The next morning I dragged myself out of bed and tried to hide my puffy eyes under cold water and a quick shower. Paul brought me coffee and set it by the sink. Neither of us could talk. I dressed Kat in a plaid smocked dress and a red sweater. I brushed her hair until it was smooth as silk and pulled it back with red bows. Paul fed her while I frantically tidied the house, not wanting to stop moving for a second.

The time came. I sat on our front porch and looked down the street for the yellow school bus with the handicapped sign. It pulled up a few minutes late. I wheeled Katherine out in her stroller. When the burly driver stepped off the bus and moved her quickly onto the platform, I felt as if I was giving her away forever. I watched the bus pull away from the curb, swerve into the flow of traffic, and drive out of sight. At that moment, I knew how difficult it would be for me ever to free myself from Katherine. We had a connection, the deepest of all bonds. How could I ever give up my lovely creation, no matter how flawed? How could I live my life if Katherine weren't a part of it?

I stopped by at lunch. Smells of mashed peas and potatoes filled the lunchroom. I remember the children's crooked teeth and cavernous smiles. Some of the older children lumbered around the room trying to help, talking in deep, halting voices. Already, Matilda—with chopped-off black hair and slobber down her chin—had adopted Kat. She stood behind Kat's high chair stroking her head, saying, "Kat pretty. Kat pretty."

I began to walk on a high desert plateau. During patterning, I held to a fragile strand of hope. I had wrapped Katherine in my arms and psyche. Her successes were my successes; her failures, my failures. My life rested on the accomplishments of her day. When we stopped, the hope died. I looked straight ahead so I wouldn't be diverted by the barrenness. I put one foot in front of the other. I let no one know how scared I was. With that first bus ride, I began disentangling myself from her. It was the hardest thing I have ever done.

The afternoon of Kat's first day, I got a call from Transportation: "You'll need to get a wheelchair for your daughter. The stroller isn't sturdy enough."

I hung up, went into Kat's room, and sat in the corner looking at the pastel flowers on her wallpaper and the mattress on the floor. No longer would baby things work for her. We couldn't hide her problems behind strollers and Huggies. We had clung to that shred of normalcy and had avoided buying anything that smacked of long-term disability. Buying a wheelchair would push us where we had never wanted to go.

With my finger in the yellow pages, I called wheelchair shops all over Denver. By the end of the day, I had located a chair that would work for Katherine. I picked it up the next morning—an oversized stroller, collapsible, but sturdy and big enough to seat a small adult. We bought a special denim insert that made it fit Katherine securely. Still it swallowed her up.

The next day, she looked tiny and forlorn sitting in her big wheelchair as the ramp rose and she disappeared into the bus. I walked back to the chaotic welcome of Helen and Alice with the image of Katherine forever tied to the wheelchair. The finality of the image stuck with me. Kat's first days of school held no sense of new beginnings.

I stopped writing in my journal. Three weeks—three years—wouldn't solve anything. I would need to be stronger than I ever thought I could be, stronger than I'd been with patterning, when hope had given me the enthusiasm of desperation. With no hope, I needed a strength not tied to dreams.

After patterning, I threw myself into work. My former boss and I started a small law firm that permitted me to work part-time. We did legal work, but I found myself more engrossed in my work with the organization to improve the public schools, particularly for inner-city kids who had few opportunities. I needed a new cause, one that challenged me and gave me a place to put all of the energy I'd devoted to Katherine. My law partner had four children. I had three. Education was a good fit, and patterning had taught me that I worked best for causes I believed in.

In the evenings I'd feed Kat, clean her, and put her to bed, brushing my lips quickly across her forehead and going on to play with Helen and Alice. Seeing Kat's thin body and crossing eyes left me empty. For too long, every minute spent with Katherine had been devoted to changing her, fixing her, making her whole. I found it impossible to relax around Katherine. Once the fixing stopped, I didn't know how to have a relationship with her. I could care for her, but I couldn't simply be with her. I didn't know what that looked like.

Each morning I scrubbed Kat's face, decorated her hair, and dressed her in matching tops and bottoms. Even as I began to distance myself from her emotionally, she looked lathered in love.

I tried to create a comfortable spot on the rim of my heart for Kat—a place I could control and keep from erupting too often. I gave up on her in a fundamental way. She let me down. I let her down.

"I think we should have another child," I told Paul in the fall of 1985.

He looked at me in disbelief. "You must be crazy, Susan. Aren't things complicated enough?"

I searched desperately for ways to cope with the pain of facing life with Katherine always a baby. I thought if we had another baby in the house, we'd need all the gear anyway—the diapers, wet wipes, baby food, high chair. When I looked at all of those things and knew they were for Katherine, then six, it left empty spaces in my heart. I wondered how to patch those holes. I didn't know. My gut was all I had as a guide, and it said the joy of a baby would ease the loss.

In the move to integrate disabled with normal children, the Denver Public Schools decided not to maintain a school devoted to the handicapped students. They closed Boettcher. The teachers were farmed out to classrooms for the disabled in elementary schools throughout Denver. I had a sinking feeling. I knew how cruel children could be and wondered who would protect Katherine from the normal kids.

In the fall of 1985, Kat went to a regular elementary school near Stapleton Airport, far from my office. At the end of a long hallway, they had a special room for the handicapped. When I went to meet the principal, he didn't make eye contact. Clearly, he had more important people to deal with than the mother of a brain-injured child. Elsewhere in my life, at least I was taken seriously. There, like Katherine, I was a second-class citizen.

At home we worked hard on potty training. If Katherine could at least do that, it would simplify our lives and help maintain her dignity. An aide at the school had a special toilet she wanted to sell cheap. She showed me a picture. It was big with a metal frame and large white seat. I couldn't bring myself to buy something that looked so final. Instead, Paul cut out and carefully sanded a circle in an old wooden high chair, making an unobtrusive potty for Katherine.

Pain pierced my side. It was June 25, 1986. The throbbing felt different from the intense but neatly spaced contractions I'd remembered with the girls. The ache turned excruciating when I tried to walk. I gave up and lay as still as possible on the hospital bed.

The doctor arrived several hours later. As he felt my stomach, I explained, "It's not like contractions. It feels like a knife is sticking between my ribs."

The doctor's casual demeanor quickly changed. He moved into action. He warned I might need a C-section, but first they'd try to induce. He added something about the placenta.

For hours I drifted in and out of a daze of pain. The contractions came closer. I had the uncontrollable urge to have a bowel movement, then I heard Mark's first cry. I held him limply in my arms as he drank from my breast, relishing those first moments but feeling an exhaustion so deep I couldn't move. Desperate for sleep, I asked the nurse not to wake me that night to feed him.

I learned later the placenta had pulled away from my uterine wall. If the doctor hadn't acted quickly, Mark could have died. I dreamed of Mark in a dark, warm ocean floating in a white translucent ball, drifting farther and farther from shore until he was out so far there was no way he could come back.

The next morning I woke with a throbbing that started in the upper part of my spine, then lodged in my temples and across my forehead. I couldn't bend my neck. Sitting up brought a flood of nausea. My temperature began to climb. A neurologist was called in.

After a spinal tap, the doctors told me I had viral meningitis. They thought the baby would be okay, but there were dangers. I could have infected Mark in utero or as he passed through the birth canal. He needed to be watched carefully. He could suffer brain damage, hearing loss.

The long watch began. Mark's temperature rose. I felt the terror of being struck by lightning twice. I knew it could happen again and believed I had been born under an unlucky star. I couldn't keep my own children safe. The excitement of having a new baby was replaced by a deep and paralyzing despair. I was told I shouldn't breast-feed. We gave Mark formula. I pumped the milk from my breasts and threw it down the sink.

I wondered why I had wanted this child so much. What void did I think it would fill? Having a baby in the house somehow eased the pain from Katherine. With patterning over, we'd turned a corner: Helen and Alice made things better, not worse. They helped us deal with our loss of a "normal" Katherine. Another child would help that much more, I had told myself. But I knew if there were something wrong, Paul would never forgive me. I'd never forgive myself.

Mother again came out to help. We took turns sleeping in the single bed next to Mark's crib. A June heat wave set in—day after day of temperatures over 100 degrees Fahrenheit. Every hour, we checked to see if his fever had broken and held his tiny flushed body in our arms rocking him back and forth. My mouth stayed dry no matter how much I drank.

After a couple of weeks, Mark's temperature was normal and he seemed fine, but for months I watched his every move. I desperately wanted to believe he was well, but couldn't relax as he reached the small milestones to health. Katherine had made me believe anything could happen.

Mark was six months old. Paul lay beside me on our bed. "God, I wish I could cry," he said. "I feel our love slipping away. It's hard to have romance with dirty bottoms constantly needing a change."

My body tightened. He was getting too close to the truth. Our trip to San Francisco before Mark had been a Band-Aid for our wounded marriage. The hurt was still very much there. We put on a cheerful front playing with the children, but we hardly spoke. I left him at night as much as he left me. I felt more alone with him than by myself. In our guest room, in the middle of the night, I ate Mint Milano cookies and escaped to *The Lord of the Rings*, Ellis Peters's mysteries, and *The New Yorker.*

"I have this horror that the thing I loved most—being in the out-of-doors—took Kat from me. Now I feel you leaving, too," Paul said, staring at the ceiling.

"Why did you give her that water? You rush through things. Why couldn't you have been more careful?"

"Sue, we don't know what caused Kat's problem. It might've been the water. It might've been something else. Don't blame me."

"I blame you and I blame myself. I shouldn't have let you do it. I should have protected Kat."

"We don't know, Sue. We really have no idea what happened with Katherine. We can guess all we want, but all those doctors couldn't figure it out. How can we? We've got to do the best we can with what we've got now. What else can we do?"

I put my head on his chest and draped an arm over his shoulder. He would always be there for Kat, and in his own way, for me. I knew I would always love him for that. But I wasn't sure I could handle the loneliness that gnawed at me when we were together and the broken dream of the relationship that could have been, but for Katherine. When we'd married, I'd believed we could go anywhere and be anything. I didn't have a clue what we were getting into.

~

At the end of a busy day at the office, I stood in the kitchen preparing dinner. Helen and Alice fought over a toy in the sunroom. Kat sat near them, oblivious to their bickering. Mark lay in the small antique crib in the living room. The week had been crazy with too many early morning and evening meetings. Paul was in Montana on business. Helen and Alice greeted me each day complaining about the babysitter. "She won't let us suck our thumbs, Mom. She's really mean."

I carried Kat upstairs to change her, then started reading *The Little Red Hen* to Alice until Helen rushed up yelling, "Something's burning, Mom. The kitchen's full of smoke."

I bolted down the steps, grabbed the frying pan off the burner, and doused it in the sink. I pulled a frozen pizza out of the fridge and threw it in the oven, then started scouring the pan caked with burned lemon chicken. Mark started crying. I plopped him in the Snugli, coated the pan with Comet, and scraped the Brillo pad firmly across the black crust. Suddenly, I stopped and held tightly to the side of the sink. The children's voices faded. I held tighter and tighter to the stainless-steel edge, gripped by a terrible fear that if I ever moved, I would break into a million pieces.

I don't know how long I stood there. Helen's "Mom, I think the pizza's ready" snapped me out of my terror. I moved my hand and it didn't break. I grabbed the pizza out of the oven with the hot pad and my whole body stayed in one piece. I knelt and wrapped Helen and Alice in my arms as Mark slept in the Snugli.

A dream recurred around this time. I sit in an exam room. Long-tubed fluorescent lights shine overhead. I take three deep breaths, then tear the gray tab locking the contents of the test with my thumbnail. A nasal voice drones, "You may now begin. You have three hours to complete the examination. Please keep your eyes on your own work."

My hands shake as I open the packet. The top of the page says "Advanced Organic Chemistry." I thought I was there for an English test. I look around. The others are marking answers with sharp number two pencils. I can't stop shaking. My head swims. Panic grabs my chest as I see the others bend their heads intently over their tests. I'm not prepared. I don't know what to do. I can't ask for help. I can't even speak.

I wake with a shudder, relieved when I find myself in bed, buried in covers, safe and protected, not needing to find a way out. But the dream doesn't fade—the fear, the helplessness, the feeling that nothing in my life has prepared me for what's ahead. There's no way out. It leaves me shaken. I realize how much I like to be in control, to know what's coming. I'm terribly afraid when success can't be achieved by just working hard.

I could dress Kat in pretty clothes, fix her hair, hug her, smile at her, and pretend. No one could see inside, but I knew. If I couldn't love this child I had created, what was wrong with me? On the outside, I looked smooth and together. Inside, I felt like the student in that exam hall who had never taken organic chemistry.

We move beyond bitterness, beyond anger, beyond broken dreams. The path winds, circling up and around. At moments we know we can't get there. We don't have it in us. The pain is too raw. We keep going. Finally, we arrive at that place—which once felt impossibly distant—where we embrace what we didn't choose.

CHAPTER 9

Photo by Paul Phillips

Holly Orona and Katherine, winter 1988.

Once I asked all the people in a workshop to close their eyes for a moment and let an image rise. It could be any image: something that flitted through their minds driving to the conference, something small that had touched their lives, something that sat at their core. After a few minutes, I looked out across the room and it was flooded with tears.

RITA, THE DOTING GRANDMOTHER, had pictures of Katherine in every room. The pictures showed Kat at every stage. At two, fragile and pretty in a white cotton dress, Kat looks down at the camera with a shy smile. At three, she lies on a red pillow on the brick patio wearing a plaid smocked dress and a beaming smile. In another, she and Helen sit on my lap. Helen grins at the camera; Kat's eyes cross and spit drips down her chin. In one family portrait, Alice, three at the time, holds down Kat's hands so she won't put them in her mouth.

At home I hid pictures from view. I threw them in a large plastic box and stored it on the top shelf in my closet. Several times I decided to organize the clutter. I'd start the process and stumble across a picture of Kat "before," looking bright-eyed at the camera with a big grin. I'd stop and put the pictures aside again.

One night I flipped through the photos in the quiet of the sleeping house, searching for something I couldn't define. I looked at every shot, forcing myself not to turn away. Somehow, it was as if I hadn't lived those years when Kat drifted from us to a world so difficult to touch. It was as if I were observing my life going by, but having no part in it. If I could have washed my mind of those images of her change, I might have been able to forget and accept Kat as she was. But the images rose randomly but inevitably like bubbles on a pond, trying to make me let them in.

For months, Mark woke us with hunger cries every few hours. Helen and Alice climbed in our bed with the bad dream excuse. We carried one back to her room only to be awakened by the other crawling in. By morning, we were zombies. Only after we'd plied ourselves with caffeine could we muster the energy to feed and dress Kat, then seven, and get her on the 6:45 AM bus. Everyday life was becoming too much to manage.

One day at work I started making calls about respite care. The next day, Linda Orona, our secretary, came into my office. Linda, a tall, graceful woman with large brown eyes, smooth skin, and dark hair, projected an air of calm and order and always remained unflappable.

"I couldn't help but overhear you yesterday," she said. "I didn't say anything then. I wanted to check with David first. We would love to help care for Katherine." They'd been looking for a family service project. Her children, Holly and Nathan, were ten and eleven. Linda wanted to get to know Katherine better, and David was happy to help out. Quietly, their act of kindness began.

Behind the Oronas' house was a small sledding hill. When we arrived to pick up Katherine, we found her wrapped in a plaid blanket sitting on a plastic sled with Nathan's arms wrapped around her. I watched as they took off down the hill. At the bottom, David picked her up and carried her up the hill to where Holly waited. He placed Katherine between Holly's legs, tucking the blanket around her hips. The two girls made the run together, broad smiles across their faces.

I watched the scene stunned by the Oronas' ability to accept Kat exactly as she was, shocked that others could bring such joy to Katherine and take such joy from her. We could never do that.

"She has been wonderful," Linda said. "We've had such fun with our dear Katrina."

On my desk is a picture of Nathan—a smart skinny kid with braces—holding Katherine's knees as she sits on a stool. Holly—a pretty girl with long, dark hair—sits on a chair behind Katherine braiding Kat's hair.

One weekend a month, they cared for Kat. They welcomed her to their home as if she were the queen. They took her to movies, athletic events, the swimming pool, the mall. They bathed her and massaged lotion over her thin body. They gave her clothes for Christmas and hand-made cards for Valentine's Day. They set a place for her at their table and made a bed for her in the middle of their den. When we picked up Katherine on Sunday afternoons, she smelled like lilac and looked like she'd been to a spa.

One day Linda told me she needed to leave the Public Education and Business Coalition, the nonprofit organization to improve public education that I'd cofounded and now directed. By then our Literacy Project worked with elementary school students, immersing them in quality literature and getting them to write every day. We awarded $500 minigrants to teachers to encourage classroom creativity. The work had grown much more time-consuming. Linda wanted to work fewer hours so she could spend more time with her children. Quickly, she also said, "We still want Kat on weekends. We couldn't let her down; besides, we'd miss her too much."

After she'd helped with Kat for three years, Linda called and told me she needed to talk. We sat in a restaurant with black and white tile floors and art nouveau posters on white walls.

"David and I are splitting," she said, tears in her eyes.

"What?" I asked, thinking I had misunderstood.

"We were good at hiding things. We've stayed together for the children. But there's no sense in that anymore. I'm moving away. I'm not sure where yet, but I'll be gone in a month. I'll take the children, of course. We'll miss Katherine. She is one of the hardest things to leave."

Linda's gift grew in my eyes when I realized she'd continued to care for Katherine in spite of her own struggles. Always, she'd made me feel that I was doing her the favor.

When she and the children moved, I felt a huge void

in my life and a deep sadness for Kat. I can only imagine how much Kat missed them.

My friend Rosa calls Kat her guru. One evening we were at her house and I found Rosa sitting on the wooden floor in her living room, hugging Kat, talking on the phone, crying. The friend on the phone had breast cancer and had just decided to undergo more intense chemotherapy. "Kat eases my fear," Rosa said.

Rita lugged Kat to the high chair, bumping her legs against the carpet like a rag doll, and hoisted her into the chair. The tray and metal tubing glistened from a recent Windex wipe down. She pulled out a plastic bib covered with rocking horses for Kat to wear and then brushed Kat's hair until it was smooth, soft, and pulled back in a thick ponytail. She began with applesauce and orange juice, talking to Kat about her week. "Sweetie, my arthritis is slowing me down a little, but at least I hiked on Mount Nystrom with the ladies on Tuesday. Did you have a good week at school? I bet they love you there."

She moved on to peas and a chicken potpie she carefully mushed before each bite. Kat ate, spitting the peas on the black garbage bags Rita had spread beneath the high chair. Rita's constant chatter went on the whole time. Kat giggled, spitting out more peas. After the chocolate pudding, the cleanup ritual began. With a clean, warm cloth, Rita wiped carefully between each finger, polished Katherine's face, and brushed her teeth three times.

"Now the best part, my little Kat," Rita said as she dragged Katherine to the living room sofa with the view of Byers Peak. Rita wrapped her arms around Kat's shoulders, pulled Kat's legs over her lap, and continued the gentle conversation that had begun long before at Mercy Hospital.

Rita had nuns in convents throughout the country praying for Kat. She had her old black nanny praying for Kat. She got everyone she knew to pray for Kat. An Ann Landers column about the hidden gifts of a Down syndrome child hung on her fridge next to the shopping lists and inspirational prayers.

"Are you bringing Kat?" she always asked when they invited us to visit in Winter Park. When we said she'd be at the Oronas', she'd try to hide the tint of disappointment. "Oh, I understand. Maybe next time it will work out."

Every winter my parents came out to ski. They'd stay with us en route to the slopes. One morning when they were leaving, I bathed Kat early, washed her hair, and pulled it back in a thick braid crowned by a pink polka-dot bow. I put a dab of perfume behind her ears. Starting at her feet, I dressed her in pink socks, pink-and-purple tennis shoes, thick pink stirrup pants, a pink-and-white-striped turtleneck, and an oversized pink sweatshirt. This once, I wanted them to notice Kat.

I sat Kat in the sunroom's overstuffed chair where she couldn't be missed. She looked fresh and pretty—no bad smells, no disheveled hair.

They didn't acknowledge her—no morning greetings. Though they wouldn't be back for a year, once again my parents left without a good-bye to Kat. They weren't deliberately cruel, just oblivious to a grandchild who couldn't give back in a normal way.

Many times I wanted to scream, "Don't you see Katherine? Can't you see her there? How can you act as if she doesn't exist?" I wanted to shake their shoulders, look them straight in the eye, and say, "She's worthy of tenderness. She asks for so little."

I don't think they knew how much I needed them to embrace Katherine, to open their hearts to her. I needed that for myself as much as for Katherine. My greatest fear was that no one else could love Kat. Thankfully, Rita and the Oronas showed me how wrong I was. Again and again they displayed an attention and adoration that brought out Kat's innocence and beauty. Again and again they showed me how lovable Katherine really was.

But I had always tried to please my parents. And their reaction to Kat made me feel as if I had disappointed them in the most profound way. I needed their support. I don't think they realized that the tables had turned: Now,

I needed them to please me by being kind and loving toward Kat. I didn't know how to tell them that. I could only respond with a silence that hid the daughter they once knew.

When we honor our lives completely—the good, the bad, the ugly—our stories grow intensely human.

CHAPTER 10

Mary Jane and Keith (Susan's parents), Paul, Katherine,
Susan, Mark, Alice, and Helen, summer 1988.

*All losses are part of a giant puzzle. If we can put the pieces
together—sharing our pain so that it connects with the pain of
others—we are somehow liberated from our personal sorrow.
Our pain doesn't go away, but it changes and hurts less. The
puzzle, once completed, never looks like it did before the loss.
It is thicker, tougher, more jagged around the edges.*

N ANCY GRAHAM called as I sat in my office writing a grant proposal. Her name rang a dim bell. She reminded me she'd been a therapist at the rehab center where I'd taken Katherine five years before.

"I've thought about Katherine all these years," Nancy said. "She was unlike any other child I've worked with. I couldn't forget her eyes."

Nancy told me about an article she'd read the day before. "It was about something called Rett syndrome. The description reminded me of Katherine. There's an address here for the International Rett Syndrome Association. You could write for more information."

A couple of weeks later, on a gray snowy day, materials from the association arrived. I didn't have time to open the packet until late in the evening after all four children were in bed. Kat was seven and a half. Paul sat beside me on the bed, reading. I tucked the down comforter around me and leaned back on a couple of pillows with the packet in hand.

The tears started. Paul looked over at me. "What's wrong, Sue? What's the matter?"

"God, Paul, I think we finally know what happened to Katherine."

I read every word while tears streamed down my face. As I finished, I handed portions to Paul.

The children described were Katherine—from the grinding teeth to the blue feet, from the constipation to the hand-wringing, from the eye crossing to the curved spines, from the normal beginning to the downward spiral somewhere between six and eighteen months of age. Katherine's picture was painted on every page.

I remembered the despair I felt as Katherine lost the use of her hands and realized, as I read, that nothing I could have done would have prevented it. I thought of the trips to the dentist to keep making new mouth guards that would prevent Katherine from grinding her teeth away; now I saw that teeth grinding was standard. The crying at night, the change from being a chubby, responsive baby to being a skinny, profoundly retarded seven-year-old— for the first time, it all fit.

An Austrian doctor, Andreas Rett, spent years working in an institution for the handicapped in Vienna. One day he went into the waiting room and saw three girls sitting next to their mothers. All of them sat with their backs hunched, wringing their hands and staring vacantly out of huge eyes. It clicked. He saw the pattern.

He reviewed their records and learned all three were normal at birth. Something unexplained had happened to them at about one year. That was 1965. Not until 1983 did an article about Rett syndrome appear in an English journal. Kat was born in 1979. It was no wonder that we'd known nothing for so long.

As I read, relief tinged with a piercing despair engulfed me. Everything I read fit Katherine. Paul and I were absolved of our guilt about the drink of water. But nothing changed. The material said there was no known cause and no known cure. There were no laboratory tests to confirm a diagnosis. There was no genetic marker, though because it had occurred only in girls, doctors suspected an X chromosome link.

After all the years, we had a label for Katherine's condition; but having a name didn't change our lives. When we told friends, they said we must be pleased to finally know. But Katherine was Katherine.

Learning of Kat's diagnosis led me to the realization that I carry a rotten seed—something out of my control, something microscopic, but essential. Driving to work, washing dishes, lying in bed waiting for sleep, it hit—a germ of an idea, a fleeting, sick thought, a deep perception that something in me was so wrong that I created Katherine.

After I learned about Rett syndrome, this thought burrowed into my mind. So little was known, yet all signs indicated a genetic link. It affected only girls. With identical twins, both had it; with fraternal twins, one did and one didn't.

I began to fear for my other children and what I might have passed to them. When I believed encephalitis had caused Katherine's problems, the weight of responsibility shook my roots and broke my heart; but I saw it as an isolated fluke, an accident, not something that would haunt us beyond Katherine's life. Rett syndrome absolved Paul and me of direct responsibility but left us with something scarier, less in our control.

I looked at Helen—elegant, vulnerable Helen—and feared she would be the one. I looked at Alice—feisty, tough Alice—and feared her daughter's Rett syndrome would break her. I looked at Mark—gentle and good-natured—and feared his smile would dim under life's tragic turn. I, like my mother, can do nothing to prevent a bolt of lightning from hitting them.

When I think about someday getting the phone call, "Mom, I'm pregnant," I will hear its bittersweet message. By then, there will be no gender surprises. They will know for months whether the baby is to be a boy or a girl. I will wish for boys, though my girls have brought me deep joy. I don't want to watch the baby mercilessly for any signs in her first year.

If there is by then a genetic marker, what would I advise? Can I stand knowing what lies ahead and do nothing? Can I stand doing something, knowing what lies ahead?

The Public Education and Business Coalition made it beyond the shaky start-up years and was thriving. I had left law practice and was the PEC's executive director. Our annual fund-raising luncheons filled the downtown Marriott. We'd undertaken a major media campaign with the *Rocky Mountain News* and KUSA Channel 9 to increase awareness of key education issues. As the PEC grew, the demands of the job changed. What had once been a part-time endeavor became very full-time.

At home my love for Helen, Alice, and Mark sustained me. But at this point I lived a treadmill life, unable to know tranquillity if I saw it. I continued my runs on Seventh Avenue, but often even they failed to calm me.

The week we'd stopped patterning, we removed all the strange contraptions from our basement den: the patterning table, the crawl box, the overhead ladder. Within a month, we had recarpeted and ordered a sectional sofa to cover up the traces of those years. Nonetheless, two years later, I found it hard going into that room. Always, I carried images of Katherine and our failed hopes for her.

We outgrew 730 Josephine. We spent hours with Realtors looking at houses in our city neighborhood. I looked with a kind of desperation, more than the usual house hunter's bug. It wasn't just that we needed more space. Our house held too many memories. I had to get out of that place where I had fought for a normal life for Kat, and lost.

Our discouragement grew as we found several perfect houses only to realize how large the gap was between our desires and our pocketbook.

On a sunny Saturday in March 1987, we visited friends in a small mountain neighborhood thirty minutes west of Denver. We admired their mountain view, not for a moment thinking we'd join them in their retreat from city life. We liked bookstores, the Sunday *New York Times*, and old movies.

They mentioned a house for sale nearby, one of the few in the neighborhood big enough for our family. Houses were rarely on the market up there. They called a Realtor neighbor who took us to see it.

The house perched on a steep hillside, a rambling, funny-looking place with an asphalt shingle roof, steep wooden steps down to the front door, a cockeyed garage with big red doors.

The sun had melted the snow, turning the roads into thick ribbons of mud. We slipped off our mud-covered shoes and walked into what felt like a shabby lodge at a summer camp. Gray linoleum covered the entrance hall and kitchen floors. Thick green curtains hung at the windows.

The house spoke simply but sturdily of solid lives unattached to material things. The owners had lived there twenty-five years, raising three children, basking daily in the beauty of the place, hiking for miles from their house, but not caring a hoot about interior decorating. The house stood proud, if a little threadbare, putting on no airs.

It wasn't until we walked out on the deck and looked out to the Continental Divide, stretching from north to south without a house to break the view, that I knew we'd found the place. I stood for several minutes after the others had gone inside. Snow was piled a foot deep on the deck. Several simple birdhouses were nailed to nearby ponderosa pines. The air smelled more alive than anything I'd ever imagined.

The next day we made an offer. Then our doubts began. What about the commute? All the snow? A school for Katherine? What about preschools, babysitters? The concerns came thick and fast. I thought I was crazy for trusting my gut and acting so quickly. Why couldn't we have waited a week, given ourselves time to think? I loved the spot, but the house needed lots of work.

On a snowy morning later in the week, Paul and I woke with the same idea. We had to make up our minds once and for all. We drove west through the heavy snow out Sixth Avenue to I-70. As we climbed the long, steep hill—the first thrust of the Rockies—we edged above the heavy cloud of snow to sunshine. At the turnoff, we sat awed by the view of the snow-covered mountains and glistening tree branches.

"Have you ever seen anything more incredible?" Paul asked. We sat hand in hand looking out to what we knew could be ours every morning of our lives if we chose. After that morning watching the sun hit the Divide, we never looked back.

Sometimes we need to pack up and leave. Sometimes we need to put our sadness and sorrow behind us and wake up in a

different place with no reminders. Maybe we move to a new
house. Maybe we rearrange a room. Maybe we go through
our house like a whirlwind, cleaning out and throwing
away. The day comes when we awake in the new place we've
created and instead of sadness, the memories of our sorrow
fill us with a surprising warmth.

The first night in our mountain house we didn't have curtains. The full moon kept us from sleeping. It lit the sky
like thousands of streetlamps, bringing out the outlines of
the trees and hills, creating a magic world of silhouettes.
We lay on our bed and looked out to the dark contours of
the Continental Divide.

Paul wrapped his arms around me. It feels so right, I
thought, wondering if the moon would ever again be so
huge. Somehow with the passage of time, the distance
I'd felt from Paul had narrowed. The change had
occurred tiny step by tiny step as the days came and
went. We weren't dealing with life's trials alone, but
were connected by the trials themselves. We had been
through the fire together, and that shared journey had
fused our lives in a way that was beginning to yield a
remarkable bond.

By then we expected little from Kat, whose eighth
birthday was a month away. We accepted her being there,
a quiet presence in our house. I'd learned to live with the
pain that came when I looked her way. Every now and

then, I'd stop and talk to her, surprised if I got smiles and knowing looks. I didn't expect responses.

An hour later, we were still awake from the glow of the moon and the excitement of the day. "Let's go for a walk, Paul. The children are sound asleep. They'll be fine." We threw on T-shirts and sweatpants and headed out the front door, struck by the chill of the summer night.

The moon's welcome silenced the wind. Not a dog barked. Stillness surrounded us as we meandered on the dirt road that circled below our house. We whispered and walked slowly, not wanting to break the spell. I held Paul's hand—basking in the uncanny quiet.

The walk and the moon's light washed away the tensions from the chaotic months of planning the move and keeping 730 Josephine clean for prospective buyers. Back at the new house, we lay wrapped in peace.

As I drifted to sleep, the image of the moon, quietly reflecting the sun's light, flashed through my mind. For a fleeting second, I saw that Katherine, too, possessed a haunting kind of reflected light. She, who had so few abilities, enabled us to look at life in a new light, to see ourselves and our world through different lenses. By doing nothing, she revealed our own inner weaknesses and strengths. I desperately wanted to hold onto that thought, but the image faded as quickly as it came.

Nonetheless, at some level, we had moved on and dear Kat was still with us.

When we are in the depths of pain and everything around us has become tasteless, we try to bury the images that remind us of our loss, to force them back into the box that holds our sorrow, but they erupt at unexpected times and leave us shaking. If we help them out, if we bring them forth and make them a part of our stories, finally, with time's passing, we are able to see the drama and beauty of our lives.

CHAPTER 11

PHOTO BY MONTE CABLE

Susan and Paul at the summit of Mount Huron, summer 2003.

Even if that which we care most about drifts from us, the mountains remain, the crashing of waves, the song of winds, the yellow of daffodils.

O N A GRAY day in February 1991, I returned to my office after lunch and saw, in the midst of a boring array of papers on my desk, a fax describing an Outward Bound sea kayaking course in Baja, Mexico. Through my work at the Public Education and Business Coalition, we'd formed a partnership with the Colorado Outward Bound School to provide leadership training to educators. I'd gone on my first course several months before.

I set the fax aside and started going through my pile of phone messages, but my eyes kept going back to the flimsy fax. I closed my door, sat down with my legs up on my desk, and pored over every word. After reading about whales, sand dunes, and mangroves, I called Paul. "How would you like to do some kayaking in Mexico?"

"Are you joking?" he asked.

"It's been years since we've had a real adventure. This sounds amazing. The kids love Twyla [the babysitter]. We can pay her extra. I'd love to do it."

When I gave him the details, he didn't hesitate. "It's the chance of a lifetime. Let's go for it!" he said, even though neither of us had ever been in a kayak.

We signed up for the eight-day course looking for an adventure and a romantic getaway in an exotic spot. On the flight out, we came down briefly in Guaymas, a god-forsaken landing strip in the middle of nowhere. In the hot, crowded Guaymas Airport, I spotted a tall, dark-haired guy across the room. He had broad shoulders and piercing blue eyes. He stood leaning against the wall with his arms crossed over his chest. When he waved and smiled, I thought, "Oh, brother, what have I gotten myself into?" It was Mark Udall. He more than looked the part of the director of the most successful Outward Bound school in the country.

In La Paz, we met the other instructors. Chris had the lean, sinewy look of someone who has spent his life out-doors. Jerry was tall, blond, and muscular. Then there were Luis and Cristobal, Mexican Zorbas and guides with Baja Expeditions, an outfit that created wilderness experiences for us gringos.

During the week, we kayaked seventy miles through Magdalena Bay, a slice of water off the west coast of Baja protected from the Pacific's waves by Magdalena Island. The sea blended with low islands of scrubby mangroves. There were few geologic markers. It felt as if you could kayak to eternity. The sun's intensity brought out the colors but created a glare that made distances hard to gauge. To stay cool, we dipped our bandannas in the sea and tied them over our heads, relishing the drips of water down our chests and backs.

Magdalena Bay's calm waters attract gray whales for mating and birthing. Within our first five minutes on the water, we saw spouts. As the week passed, we saw many mothers with their babies. At first, I was terrified to be sharing the water with such giants, but I came to view them as glorious, benign creatures. In the evenings, we sat on dunes, watching their colossal forms move smoothly through the waves, listening to their gushing breaths of life.

On that trip I learned that the large, obvious challenges of Outward Bound don't compare to the small, under-the-skin ones. I can paddle for eight hours straight, but I don't hold up well with sand in my sleeping bag. I can handle camping, but don't like "groovers"—metal ammo cans that serve as toilets and leave deep furrows in your rear. More than anything, I learned, once more, about shattered expectations. Near the end of the trip, we hiked for twelve hours through sand dunes and up a cactus-covered mountain. It rained hard much of the day. "I can do this hike even in the rain," I thought, "because tonight I'll have a dry tent and a warm—if sandy—sleeping bag."

On the late return to camp, when I was too tired to eat and had blisters from my wet tennis shoes, Paul and I found our tent blown over, our sleeping bags drenched, and every item of clothing covered with a thick puddle of sand and water. Even the bristles of our toothbrushes were caked with a sunscreen/sand concoction. We had no choice but to put the pieces back together as best we could. The next morning, I pulled myself out of the wet bag with a proud, but dampened, spirit. I'd been miserable, but I'd made it. At least the worst was over.

Then came "solo night." I dreaded this Outward Bound

ritual, solitary time with only a sleeping bag, a water bottle, and a journal. I figured I might be lonely and scared, but at least I'd get a peaceful sleep. As the light faded, I looked out to the sea and wrote about whales, kayaking, sunsets. I avoided thinking about Katherine, not wanting to be overcome with sorrow on that quiet night.

When the sun went down, I huddled deep in my sleeping bag and listened to the even wash of the waves against the shore. A sense of peace filled me and I was certain I'd have the calmest night of my life.

The band of coyotes that found my quiet outpost had different plans. They'd sneak up and play tug-of-war with my sleeping bag. I'd sit up and yell, madly waving my arms to scare them away, and see three or four canine figures rush into the bushes. Then I'd shake in my bag, too scared to drift off to sleep, until they'd return and we'd repeat the same routine. I lay with my eyes wide open, staring at the stars, wondering what coyotes really liked to eat. I wasn't about to blow my alarm whistle to bring the Outward Bound instructors.

The whole course reminded me of my sense of helplessness with Katherine. Each day, I would start with a good attitude, sure the worst was behind, pleased I'd managed as well as I had, and then something unexpected would set me back again.

On the final day, we rose early, ate a spartan breakfast, and broke camp. My adrenaline flow was at its peak. I washed dishes and stuffed sleeping bags with unusual fervor. For three nights, we'd looked across the channel to the enchanting lights of San Carlos—no doubt a tropical paradise, a charming village with palm trees and tall, chilled drinks. I couldn't wait for a shower and a leisurely drink in its Main Street café. Our instructors had also promised an afternoon of shopping in La Paz. The temptations grabbed my soul. I wanted to savor the memories of the whales, dunes, and sea, but I was sick of sand and wanted out of there.

The seven-mile crossing began calmly. At first we chatted and paddled with little effort. The instructors kept reminding us to stay in formation: each boat with a partner rowing parallel and close together.

About an hour out, the wind picked up. The waves grew choppy. Our kayaks began to feel like plastic boats in a child's bathtub ready to capsize with a twist of the hand. The sky remained cloudless and deep blue, but whitecaps topped the waves and the sea swirled around us. As we paddled, we encountered steeper waves and leaned into them.

An island gave some protection for about a half hour, its wind shadow calming the sea. Beyond it, we felt the full force of the wind. It was then I thought I was going to die. Outward Bound had lost several students on a sea kayaking course years before. A fluke, they said; the storm came up so fast no one knew what had hit them.

I saw the shore a couple of miles ahead. I didn't talk. I

didn't look around. I saw only the waves that tossed our flimsy boat and the place on shore I'd set as our destination. Few thoughts crossed my mind. All had to do with the children. I had so much to live for. I couldn't let them down by spending eternity at the bottom of Magdalena Bay.

In that moment, when my terror brought clear focus, I realized the child I most needed to live for was Katherine. She could not manage without me. Hers was the life that would be too changed. The others were bright and charming. They would be much loved. They would cope.

Kat would end up in an institution somewhere. She would have no place to go, no one to love her. Who would want the broken child? No one is tied to her as I am. No one can love her as I do, even though I falter at times, even though I spent years disappointed by her, even hating her at times.

I paddled harder. I looked to that spot on the shoreline and concentrated all my energy there. When we finally pulled the boats out on the rocky coast, a weight lifted. I felt a deep relief, but the uneasiness wouldn't go away. I crouched on a boulder, arms wrapped around my knees, looking out to the sea as the wind painted the wave tops white.

For the next nine hours, we sat pelted by sand on the desolate beach of San Carlos. Baja Expeditions had failed to send the transport bus. Distance alone had given San Carlos charm. Up close, it was a poor, dirty, rumpled place.

We saw cars come and go from the shack up the beach. It turned out the ramshackle structure was a cantina. Lukewarm beer and Coke quenched our thirst. I had dreamed about a real toilet to sit on, instead of a groover. The cantina's toilet was caked, waterless, just a hole down to the beach.

The smoke and smells drove me from the cantina. I built a fortification of orange crates to shield me from the blasting wind and sat on the beach bombarded by the thoughts from the week. And it wasn't over yet. I knew there'd be no shopping in La Paz, and I began to prepare mentally for another night in the tent.

In a week, I'd had what felt like a lifetime's worth of highs and lows. Yet as I leaned back against the orange crates and closed my eyes, a warmth and joy crept into my heart. I felt a soaring inside. Giggles of relief shook me. With grit in my teeth and sand thick in my hair, I understood more vividly than ever before the power that comes from enduring, and going forward, regardless of the pain, regardless of the obstacles.

We've been caught for a long time, unable to see our way through, gripped by a fear that leaves us breathless with foreboding. But the time comes when we must break through to a new state of being. An Outward Bound motto says, "If you can't get out of it, get into it." Finally, we tell ourselves, "This is it, this is my life." And we get into it. We really get into it.

⟿

In April 1991 I sat on a heavy wooden chair behind the Mabel Dodge Luhan house, a rambling adobe structure bordering Pueblo lands and looking out to Taos Mountain. Smells of sagebrush and thyme filled the air. A warm breeze blew from the west. Not a cloud marred the deep blue of the sky. I was in Taos for a conference on the arts and humanities in education.

Five weeks before, when we'd returned from Baja, we'd found Rita dying of brain cancer. I went to the Taos conference reluctantly, afraid Rita might die during that long weekend, but knowing there was nothing I could do for her. She lay semicomatose at Fitzsimmons Hospital, hooked up to tubes and a breathing apparatus.

The ironic coincidence of returning that rainy evening in Baja to a camp in disarray and then several days later returning to the real-life disarray and bewilderment of Rita's dying haunted me. Our wretched day on the beach at San Carlos was the day of Rita's brain biopsy. I didn't know how I would manage without Rita. She had loved all of the children—but especially Katherine—so completely.

The kayaking trip had tapped a side of me that I'd long buried. It had reminded me how much the wilderness filled my cup and gave me perspective on my life, showing me how little my personal ups and downs mattered in the grand scheme of things. It also brought confusion and a yearning for a footloose life I knew I could never have—not with four children, one severely handicapped. I had protected myself by suppressing my craving for adventure and spontaneity. When it came erupting to the surface, it brought turmoil and too many questions.

The first night at the Mabel Dodge Luhan house, I slept in the solarium. I climbed up steep stairs past crude geometric paintings on the risers and entered through an aqua-painted trapdoor. The curtainless room of windows gave a 360-degree panorama of Taos. I used a bathroom with a leaky pedestal tub and windows painted by D. H. Lawrence. I knew immediately I was in a remarkable place visited by phantoms from the past.

That evening we were told the ghost of Mabel Dodge—the New York socialite captivated by the New Mexico landscape and the passions of Tony Luhan, a Pueblo Indian—frequently floated down the narrow hallways of the house she'd made into a famous meeting place for the literati seventy years before.

The next day we were given the afternoon to think and write about the impact of the arts and humanities on our lives. I hadn't slowed down for months—years. I hadn't had a quiet afternoon for as long as I could remember. What would I do with myself? What might I learn?

I looked out to the sage-and-piñon-covered land of the Pueblo reservation and thought about the months leading up to that day. I could hardly move. Too much, too fast was all I could think. The peace and beauty of the Taos land crept over me. I thought how such places gently stripped away our everyday cares, peeling them back like the petals of an artichoke, and knew that if ever I were to find peace in this life, to get in touch with my inner voice, it would be through my relationship with that land, those spirits.

Then my pen took me to Katherine. I didn't want to go there. I was away with a few hours of peace. The last thing I wanted to dwell on was my life back home. I wanted to write profound thoughts about the paintings of van Gogh and Picasso, the music of Mozart and Bach, but I couldn't. That spirit-filled land had made it impossible for me to look away from the sorrow that continued to sit at the center of my life.

By then I spent little time alone with Katherine. She was always there, part of the family, but in a quiet way, a fixture in the house that people walked past, sometimes acknowledging, sometimes simply passing by. Even when she looked me straight in the eye, smiled, and "talked," I'd usually move on after a brief word or pat, unable or unwilling to take the time to really be with her. Occasionally on Friday evenings, when the chaos of the week had calmed, I'd ask myself what time I'd spent with Katherine. Inevitably, it was little.

After patterning, I didn't know what to do with Kat. She wasn't in a grade. She didn't get report cards. She didn't fit in this world that looks at what we and our children *do*—soccer, Scouts, piano, gymnastics. Kat was being, not doing. I didn't fully know it then, but she was trying to teach me to be, to hear my dreams, to listen to my breathing, to watch clouds change shape in the sky.

My obsession with fixing her, changing her, making her into something she could never be, had ruled my life and my relationship with her. I couldn't seem to understand that Kat's power came from what she reflected back to those around her, to what she evoked in them.

Keeping her at arm's length was my defense mechanism. I biked or ran every day. The other children demanded a lot of attention. I enjoyed my work, but often came home drained. I told myself keeping Katherine with us—even though I spent so little time with her—was far better than sending her to an institution. At least she was among people who loved and protected her. Sitting on that wooden chair in Taos, somehow I knew that wasn't enough.

The floodgate opened. The Outward Bound confrontations, Rita's dying, the starkness of the New Mexico landscape built up to that afternoon behind the Mabel Dodge Luhan house. They were all connected to my life with Katherine and the search she had made me undertake.

I sat, looking out to Taos Mountain, and cried for the Susan I once was, for the Susan before Katherine, for the person who walked that painful journey alone, not knowing where to turn or how to ask for help, frightened by what she knew but couldn't accept. For years the Rocky Mountain sunshine, a fresh spring breeze, the year's first crocuses, a view of the high peaks couldn't cleanse the sadness away.

I thought of Helen's music box, a gift from Paul. Together they built it, carefully sanding sides, shellacking wood, and gluing blue velvet inside. It sang a lilting "Edelweiss," then stopped suddenly in the middle of the song until Helen again twirled its key and opened its lid.

Paul and I raced through our days until the weekends came. When we stopped, sometimes we found the music. Other times we saw ourselves trapped by Kat—the presence of her splintered life always there. We found joy in the other children and in hikes on the paths near our house, but the starkness of the life ahead with a child hurt and helpless never left.

Pearl Buck wrote about two kinds of people in the world: those who have known inescapable sorrow and those who have not. The loss of Katherine couldn't be mourned and put in its proper place. The reality of feeding her, changing her, dressing her every day, the birthdays and holidays that came and went, leaving her unchanged, barred that.

I wondered why I was so tied to her, why I could never really get away or accept her as she was. I looked down the long tunnel of our lives and wondered how I could find, in our daily routine, a path to higher ground, a contentment, when I knew someday the daily chores would be too much. I had a sinking horror I would reach the end of my psychological rope before my physical one.

I wrote to the sound of the wind rustling the piñon trees. I wrote for hours as tears streamed down my cheeks and the sun beat down on my hair. I had not realized how much pain I carried and how completely shattered I continued to be by the loss of my first child. The years had passed, but the pain hadn't. I saw I couldn't escape from that beautiful, broken child no matter how much I cluttered my life. When I was left alone, my mind went to her.

Something snapped in me that day. I wondered why I had fought so long and hard against the reality of Kat's life. Why had I been so stiff? Why couldn't I have been a tree that bends in the storm, that flows with it, rather than fights against it? I had always loved the wizened old trees, twisted, frayed, and strengthened by life. My rigidity had held me back and exhausted me. There was something keeping me from moving forward—some pride or stubbornness or unwillingness to face the sadness head-on.

After that trip, each day I wrote down images that haunted me from my life with Katherine. I thought of the past: her blue doll, the activity center, the drink from the stream, the crib downstairs. I thought of the present: her birthdays, Christmases, her impact on the other children, the diapers and high chairs, the illnesses that knocked her flat and showed me how fragile she really was. I juggled the other commitments in my life and squeezed in the writing early in the morning or late at night. I'd write in the darkness with the moonshine entering the windows and remain still like a deep lake until the ripples of my memory surfaced onto the page.

That day in Taos, I realized that I could not deal with Katherine by keeping the pain at arm's length. I had to allow myself to hurt, to be angry, to feel the despair. Only if I allowed the images to emerge and then embraced them could I ever understand the mystery of Katherine and awaken those parts of me that were still numb.

How can it be that the greatest pain gives us the greatest ability to experience joy?

CHAPTER 12

PHOTO BY PAUL PHILLIPS

Mark, Helen, Katherine, and Alice, Christmas 1988.

Images that bring peace mix with images that bring turmoil, flashes from the unconscious that jump out like leaping tongues of fire. Let them out, those flames. Let them open our hearts to a new way of being.

She lay on the bed asleep.
Her perfect features
at peace.
No wrinkled brow.
No contorted lips.

She lay peaceful.
Any kid asleep
after her first day
of school.

I marvel at her beauty
at rest.
How normal she appears.

Sometimes I think
She will awaken
with stories
to tell.
Instead, she wakes trapped
A gentle spirit
in a useless shell.
Her eyes alone speak
Pleading for understanding
Dancing with pleasure.
I hope her dreams are sweet.

KAT WOULD have started junior high today. She'd
have boyfriends and pimples. She'd feel awkward
and ugly like adolescents do. She'd be profound and beautiful. She'd break hearts.

I drove by our old house at 730 Josephine. As I passed through the well-kept neighborhood with big brick houses and wide boulevards thick with flowers, I felt an overpowering urge to run away. Passing 730 Josephine reminded me of too much living. I didn't want to live so deeply and painfully anymore. I just wanted to help my seventh grader pack herself off to school. I would give anything for that—all my money, my life in a second— but I can't cut those deals, as much as I would like to.

Changing seasons hurt most, seeing that with the passage of time, Kat remains unchanged. I buy the others school supplies and wonder what's on the seventh graders' list. At Kat's school, I send the same activity fee year after year.

I laid out Helen's, Alice's, and Mark's clothes for their first school day. I had an outfit in mind for Kat but couldn't find it. I started to pull out an old sweat suit, then thought, It's Kat's first day, she should look special, too. In my closet where I'd squirreled away a couple of Kat's birthday presents, I pulled out the hot pink pants with the oversized pink-and-black-striped sweatshirt. Kat grinned broadly when I dressed her in her new outfit.

I pushed her out to her bus, greeted the bus driver, patted Kat's leg saying, "Have a good day," and thought of Kristen, a friend of Kat's when they were babies. We have pictures of them together. Kat was the pretty, alert one. Who would have guessed how each would spend her seventh-grade year—her life?

I don't want to see the seventh graders lining up to get on the bus. I'll find a quiet place to hide my eyes, and then I'll bury my dreams once more. I hope I can bury them deep enough so that the face I show to the world looks calm.

On my way to work, I listened to Dylan—"It ain't no use to sit and wonder why, babe." When the music stopped, I sat still, caught in traffic. I hadn't let the moment sink in. I'd gotten all four children off to their first days of school. Kat headed to Margaret Walters School again. With one tear's worth of sadness, I had made it through the toughest part of a day I dread every year.

A dark cloud builds several days before Katherine's birthday. Each year it hits like a hurricane. I don't want to awaken tomorrow and find Katherine lying in her bed one year older, unable to walk, talk, or feed herself. Her first screams of life ring too clearly in my head.

At the grocery store, the children picked out a chocolate cream pie and yellow candles for Kat. Tomorrow will be a busy day. Helen, Alice, and Mark go to Spanish before school and have violin lessons after. It's back-to-school night at their school. Paul leaves for a business trip. I don't know when we'll fit in a celebration.

I'll bathe Kat, dress her in a new flowered outfit, and French braid her hair. Her teacher said I didn't need to send a cake; she's baking one. For dinner, I'll feed Kat a peanut butter and jelly sandwich smothered in applesauce and softened with orange juice. The other children will sing "Happy Birthday" and fight over who gets to blow out her candles.

I rush through Kat's birthdays, hurrying to put them behind me. We never invite friends. She's never invited to birthday parties. My friend Rosa sent her a card, and my mother.

Kat lights up when I talk about her birthday. She smiles and buries her head in her pillow. She seems to know so little and so much. In the past, I've thought we were fortunate to have a child so hurt: She didn't understand enough to feel the pain of her loss. Watching Kat over the years, I think she knows and accepts. Unlike my normal children who already wish for the talents and beauties of others, Kat seems comfortable as she is.

Kat is skinny as a rail but has developing breasts and hair under her arms. No one tells you handicapped kids develop like other kids. It's just the brain that's broken. She'll start her period soon. She's moaning—a different sound. She's caught in time with a body blossoming and no mind to match. Her back is curving more; the scoliosis worsens with puberty. Kat is growing up. What is she growing into? Do I even know her, this child who rocked my life and opened my heart? I have rushed through life to avoid confronting who Kat really is and who that makes me. Little by little, I'm more able to see her as she is. Yet even now, sometimes I look at her and think there will be a miracle.

I hadn't visited Kat's school for more than ten months. I write notes every day. I thank her teachers. I want to support them, but usually my support ends at Kat's bus where day after day I bundle her up, greet her driver, push her onto the platform, and wish her a good day.

Time and again, I told myself I needed to visit. Each time I found an excuse at the last minute. Finally, I stopped early one morning on my way to work. It drizzled on the drive down the mountain, the first cold, gray day that September. My car thermometer read 39 degrees Fahrenheit.

When I arrived, Kat was propped in her standing cube. Her eyes drooped, her knees buckled. I kissed her cheek and talked to her but didn't get a response. After twenty minutes in the standing cube, an aide carried her to a huge beanbag chair where she collapsed and closed her eyes. I sat beside her and watched her classmates.

Bianca has one eye. Her nose, mouth, and eye are set on one side of her face. She sits in her wheelchair and turns her whole head to see, an innocent Cyclops trying to figure out her world.

J. R. touches everything. He extends his hand to shake, saying, "Hi." He grabs shoulders, then moves in front, again extending his hand to shake, saying, "Hi."

Lucas is a good-looking blond who seems like an average teenager until you see he can't sit still and has trouble spitting out words.

Amanda smiles, showing a mouthful of crooked teeth. She stands in a wooden contraption with Velcro straps wrapped around her legs and midriff to hold her contorted body upright.

Sharon, the gentle giant, helps the other children. She gives Amanda juice, brushes Kat's hair, and repeats, "Kat's mom. Kat's mom. Kat's mom."

There are eleven children and three adults in Kat's class. An occupational therapist worked with one child on a mat. Another girl lay asleep, a feeding tube in her stomach. The aides fed the children snacks. They played a funny "ants in your pants" tune. The children who were able danced and swayed. Those who couldn't sat looking dazed.

Tina, the occupational therapist, told me how much she enjoyed working with Kat. "Kat followed colored lights with her eyes and once reached out for a banana."

Kat's teacher, a tall, pretty woman, came over. She looked stressed at 9:30 AM. "It's the largest class in the school," she said, wiping Bianca's mouth. "But it's a great group of kids." She started telling me about each one. "People ask me how I can do my work day after day. But I can't imagine doing anything else. I love these guys."

Tears welled in my eyes. Buck up, I thought. Show her how much you appreciate her gift. Don't feel sorry for yourself, shocked at the reality you know, but don't want to face.

I looked at Kat and her classmates. It's not what I'd planned for you, Kat, I thought. But it's what we have, and what she has. She didn't look out of place. It's where she belongs. I'm not sure when I'll go back.

A friend said, "You know what, sometimes you don't have a choice. You just have to get over it."

A nineteen-year-old Swedish woman with Rett syndrome had a baby. She was too far along in her pregnancy when the doctor discovered it to abort. They found the culprit, a worker at the institution where she lived and father of two young children. He was convicted of rape and sent to prison for two years. The baby has Rett syndrome.

A sixteen-year-old handicapped girl was molested by a thirty-three-year-old man. She lived in a group home; he worked there from midnight to morning. The newspaper said he fondled her improperly, sat her on his lap suggestively, and touched her when he changed her diaper. The story left out the details. The proof was slim. She couldn't talk. She couldn't run from him. He held her captive—or could have. She wouldn't know how to protect herself. She couldn't scream.

I took Kat out to her bus. There was a new driver—a man. The usual cheerful woman had gotten a new route.

On the bus sat two brain-injured teenage boys. I put on a cheerful face, but cringed inside. Away from home, anything could happen. I would never know.

A friend told me of a child with Down syndrome who'd been institutionalized. After her death, her records showed she'd had three abortions while at the institution. The same friend also told me about a nurse walking in on a doctor, pants down to his knees, hands on a girl's shrunken shoulders. "I assure you," she said, "it doesn't matter how pretty they are."

I want to wrap Kat in my arms. I want to protect her innocence. She is beautiful and gentle and there are those who kill baby seals for their white coats. I fear for Katherine. Only Paul and I can keep her safe by keeping her here in our home surrounded by people who love her. It is our choice to make. Even now, I could be with her twenty-four hours a day if I chose. Instead, I let her out in the world. I shield her only part of the day.

The excrement Kat smeared across her neck and in her hair didn't seem to bother her. She looked at me with her beautiful, vacant eyes. After cleaning her up, I went outside and watched the night sky. A couple of planes passed overhead. Wind blew the ponderosa pines that surround our house—no sound of cars or people, simply the wind and the stars.

I shut down for a minute to lessen my anger and frustration. Those moments thrust me over the edge. I began to plan another life for Kat—a home somewhere away from us. The feedings, dressing, bathing—all someone else's burden; someone else's chore to clean her up when she vomits or her hand reaches down her diaper and spreads her waste over her body.

But then I think of my own disgust. How would someone who knew her less deal with it? With a slap across the face, a punch in the stomach? Or would they leave her in her own mess until the next morning when someone else was on duty? Kat wouldn't know the difference. Only I would be sickened by the thought.

Kat's eyes plead. She wants me to understand. I look away as she grinds her teeth and wrings her hands.

I'm not sure I want to know my options. Putting her in an institution would be, for me, a defeat. Not only could we not fix her; we couldn't fix ourselves enough to take Katherine with the flow of life—one painful wrinkle.

My hands always stink. I scrub them after changing and cleaning Kat but can't wash away the smell. I carry her with me wherever I go.

We tossed Kat's fold-up wheelchair in the back of the car and lugged her out.

"It makes things a lot more complicated," Paul said, arguing against taking Katherine with us to Mark's birthday party at the pool. "It's okay. I'll take care of her," I responded, wondering if I really wanted to.

She's heavy, around sixty-five pounds, though that's not the problem. What keeps us from taking Kat is not the weight, but something else. People stare. Their reactions force us to acknowledge just how different and how hurt Kat is.

When we take Kat to the pool, I see children her age. Their limbs are long and strong, their bodies tan, their voices high-pitched and full of play. Kat sits in her wheelchair wringing and mouthing her hands, her body skin and bones, her stare blank.

The other children laugh and run, shout and quarrel. It comes so easily. Kat sits trapped, looking nowhere, seeing who knows what. I push her into a corner out of the wind. She sits calmly wringing her hands, nodding off, waking and wringing her hands. Where are you, dear Kat?

I once took my four children and a buddy of Alice's to Tiny Town. Someone's eccentric dream, it's a Lilliputian town with miniature houses and buildings and a tiny train that takes visitors around the make-believe neighborhood.

As I pushed Kat along Tiny Town's gravel path, I noticed three boys playing. They pranced from one house to another. As Kat and I passed, they stared.

The leader of the pack pointed, started laughing, and taunted, "Look at that girl. Look at that girl." I caught his eye. He looked away and then looked back to see if my stare remained. After a minute, his friends grabbed his arm and he went back to his carefree game.

I watched as he ran off, then approached his mother.

"Is that your son?" I asked, pointing to the blond-headed child running away. She nodded.

"He made fun of my daughter. It was pretty mean-spirited. You might want to have a talk with him."

I walked on, tears forming in eyes covered by dark glasses. I caught up with my family. Helen came up and asked if she could push Kat. Alice walked over and wiped Kat's mouth.

Many people ignore handicapped children. They put them out of sight and mind. Even when some friends visit and Kat is sitting on the overstuffed library chair, they don't look her way. They avoid her eyes.

Sometimes before guests arrive, we put Kat in her room, snuggle her in bed, and hope for an early sleep. They won't have to see her and feel awkward because of her presence. They won't experience the discomfort many others have shown.

My sister-in-law visited. She'd never met Kat before. She spent five days in my house and never looked Kat's way, never said a word to her, never asked me about Kat. As the time passed, I kept thinking, Maybe today. But nothing ever happened.

I tried to ignore my parents' cold response to Katherine but felt cut off from them emotionally. They could pity Kat, mourn her loss, but they couldn't open their hearts to her. Perhaps they were at a stage in their lives when they wanted only the joy of being grandparents. That didn't include the burden of Katherine. Being around them magnified my own shortcomings. I knew too well the challenge of loving Kat.

The people I cherish don't avoid Kat. They talk to her, hold her, acknowledge her spirit. They can't know how much I love them. If I told them, they wouldn't understand. To them it is natural. They have taught me so much; it is getting easier for me, too.

Kat's frantic moans rouse me from a dream-filled sleep. I cover my head with the pillow, thinking her cries are part of my dream. Paul sleeps quietly next to me, undisturbed by Kat's frightened calls. I alone tune in to her lonesome voice in the night.

I flip on the light and find Kat kneeling, balanced precariously on the edge of her mattress, six inches off the floor. Her arms cross her chest, her hands clench in fists. She struggles, trying to keep from falling off the precipice to the plush carpet below. Her eyes open wide, her mouth purses. She dances on the edge, her body valiantly trying to protect her from the fall. Her cries for help reach out to anyone who can save her from certain disaster.

I grab her quickly in my arms. She takes a deep breath

as her body's tightness melts away. I hold her, pat her on her back, pull her covers back, and lay her gently in the middle of her double bed.

The clock reads 3:35. I remember nights when Kat was tiny. I'd awaken before her cry for food, anxious to hold her in my arms, hoping she'd wake. I remember nights during her downward spiral when the only way I could escape her haunting cries was to put her in the downstairs crib. I remember the nights throughout the years when I've lain struggling between my need for sleep and the note of terror in her lonely night cries.

If I put Katherine in a group home somewhere, I would still hear her at night. Why am I bound for a lifetime, the umbilical cord never cut?

Many Saturday mornings, I lie in bed wondering where I will find the energy to enter Katherine's room, greet her, reach down to hug her, strip off her clothes, clean her bottom, carry her into the bathroom, ease her into the warm water, lather her body with soap, and shampoo away the cares of the week.

Kat's mattress sits on the light-brown carpet in her small room. A small closet holds all of her folded clothes. Another closet stores her coats and dresses. There are no chests, no chairs. A brightly colored afghan rests at the end of her bed. My sister stenciled flowers on the white walls with borders at the ceiling and floor of winding green vines and pink tulips. Bluebirds, redbirds, yellow butter-flies, and hundreds of little brightly colored rosebuds complete the room.

Sometimes when I enter, I find Kat awake with a Mona Lisa smile, shockingly at peace. At those moments, it is as if her room is a flower garden and she is a beautiful, silent flower blooming in it.

Other times, she wakes agitated—her long dark hair a shambles—caught in the world of eye crossing and teeth gritting.

Saturday mornings, the unending nature of the routine hits. On those days, when I slow down, the pain catches up.

People talk about finding a good service project—not "make work," but something real that makes a difference. I listen and never speak, but I think how lucky I am because I have a built-in, day-in-day-out service project. It is so basic and so real, my service project.

I shave Kat's pubic hair. I tell myself it's because it makes her easier to clean. Really, it's to keep her a child. I cringe at the long, dark hairs that grow under her arms. I have no reason to shave those away. I dress her in long sleeves. Only briefly in the morning when I change her or bathe her does the reality of that woman's hair hit me.

I started shaving her when the diaper changing

became a greater chore. Shaving her smooth made sanitary sense. Even more, it kept her a little girl who will someday grow up. I've already acknowledged the falseness of my dreams. I don't need the physical reminder of Kat's fate. The incongruity of a diaper on a teenager with curling, thick pubic hair shocks me, even after many years of coming to accept what Kat's life holds.

When I bathe Kat, I marvel at the imperfection of my creation. She splashes and purrs, drawn into the warm womb of the calm water. She moves her head back and forth, relishing the swishing water where she is less inhibited by her broken body. Her feet turn out. Her soft, skinny legs, like the legs of an old man, stiffen, then relax. When she splashes her face, she winces, closing her eyes tightly, waiting to be understood.

Kat shows me every day where I'm headed, where we're all headed. Her limbo has just been longer. I pray for the day Kat will be freed from her body. I picture her spirit soaring to mountaintops. I don't believe in an afterlife. Yet I believe in her spirit and goodness. I believe someday she will appreciate the sunset and the mountain wildflowers.

I lift Kat carefully from the bath, one hand under her neck, the other at her knees. In one quick hoist, I lift her from the water to the waiting towels. First I wrap her whole body in terry cloth. Then I gently pat her, starting with her feet and stopping at her bottom. Always a thin stream of brown drips down, leaving a spot of brown on the towel. With a Kleenex, I wipe her carefully then diaper her quickly, hiding the reminder of her age and the years ahead.

Those losses that cause the most pain, those challenges that leave our hearts tied in knots and our mouths dry, those things we most dread can be our greatest opportunities. They take us places we never expected to go. They open unimaginable vistas. They allow us to find our own path.

CHAPTER 13

Paul Sr. and Rita's fiftieth wedding anniversary, summer 1990.

We write to embrace our pain—to express the power of our denial or the force of our anger. We write as we cry—calmly or violently—looking out to the mountains or sea or houses or high-rises that surround us. We write so that we can view our sorrow as a story, one story among billions.

R ITA WORE the most ridiculous hats. She had a bright red Zorro hat that tied under her chin, pillbox hats with veils, straw hats with huge brims, Australian outback hats. In a time when hats were passé, Rita continued the fashion, oblivious to the rest of the world.

In the summer, when the thermometer hit the high nineties, Rita visited us wearing long sleeves and stockings, complaining of the heat. I never saw her in shorts or a bathing suit. She'd go for a walk in the winter, piling one sweater on top of another, then topping them off with an oversized down coat. She bought shoes several sizes too big and layered socks. Not a square inch of skin was left uncovered.

Her closets were works of art: bottles of Listerine stacked in rows; Colgate, Crest, and Vaseline jars in neat lines; bomb shelter closets with provisions to last a lifetime and beyond. I marveled at the order behind those closed doors. When she wasn't home, I'd open the closet doors just to admire them.

In February 1991 Paul Sr. and Rita headed for an Elderhostel in Arizona. On the drive south, Rita began dropping things with her right hand. She didn't feel well. After a couple of days, she and Paul Sr. headed back to Colorado. She entered the hospital for tests.

They'd planned to babysit for a weekend while Paul and I were on the sea kayaking trip to Mexico. When Paul

Sr. called to let us know Rita was at Fitzsimmons Hospital and they wouldn't be able to help that weekend, we arranged other babysitters and didn't think much of it.

Paul Sr. called periodically to let us know how the tests were going. Everything sounded routine. We busily threw together our gear in preparation for the trip.

We left on a Friday with everything under control. An hour after we returned ten days later, Paul got the call from his dad. "Your mother has brain cancer. They've just done a biopsy. She's still unconscious."

The next day, Paul's call came in the middle of a meeting. "Grab a taxi and get out here as quick as you can. She's dying."

Rita lay comatose in the emergency room with a breathing tube stuck down her throat. After the surgery, her brain had swelled. They didn't know if she'd make it to morning.

On our drive home from the hospital, Paul crumpled in the front seat with an overpowering pain in his gut brought on by the fear he'd missed his chance to tell his mother good-bye.

Rita revived from the coma, but she was never the same. During our first few visits, she communicated a little. She smiled when we told her about the children and always asked, "How is my sweet Katherine?"

Then she got grumpy. Nothing pleased her. She hated the room. She spoke randomly about moving to a hospice. She feared leaving this world. She wanted to see her grandchildren grow up. Paul Sr., her husband of fifty years, lived with her at the hospital for those last hopeless months. He did everything he could for her. At first he arranged for radiation treatments and physical therapy. Then, as her condition worsened, he stayed by her bed, feeding her and making sure she was getting all the medication she needed.

During World War II, Paul Sr. was captured by the Japanese in the Philippines. For four years, he was a prisoner of war. Rita wrote him every day. She didn't know if he was alive or dead, but she kept writing. Many of her letters found him. "Those letters kept me alive," he once told me, and I thought of that conversation as he tended Rita, returning to her what she had once given him.

Rita drifted further away until we'd sit by her side whispering in ears that heard nothing. Each visit, she seemed a little more like Kat.

Rita had spent hours with the children doing crochet and needlepoint. She'd watch their plays and applaud as if she'd seen the best of Broadway. She came laden with packages at Christmas, Easter, and birthdays. Always she brought as many for Kat as for the others. She'd struggle to get Kat up on her lap, then hold her chatting nonstop. When Rita visited, Kat greeted her with an impish grin. They shared a secret. Kat would never tell.

I bathed Rita a month before she died. She could still talk a little. She seemed grateful for the gentle caresses and the smooth cloths wiping her tired body. She was relieved when the orderlies left her to the privacy of relatives. She leaned back, floating in the deep tub. Every now and then she'd open her eyes and look at me and I'd think how much we had gone through together.

Toward the end, she stopped eating. Her body closed down. Everything about her seemed dry—like a leaf blown off an autumn tree. She slept round-the-clock in the small, private room whose green walls were covered with get well cards and pictures the children had drawn.

We never took Kat to see her. Now I think we should have. Maybe Kat could have understood and communicated with Rita on a level we couldn't. When Rita died, one of Kat's few friends died. We all miss her, but Kat was left the loneliest.

In July 1991 I was in Leadville, Colorado, for another Outward Bound course. On the van ride to "The Rock," a cliff at Camp Hale—the mountain valley where the famed Tenth Mountain Division trained during World War II—I thought about all that had happened in my life since my first climbing day eight months before.

The ache from Rita's absence remained. When Paul Sr. visited, Katherine looked around as if she were trying to find something and then settled down with a frightened, lonely look on her face.

The Baja trip had inspired me to try new things and

to push my limits, but also to move on when things collapsed, shattered by events out of my control.

Since Taos, writing about Katherine had brought tears combined with a curious calm as I tapped into the raw core I needed to confront, especially as Katherine grew older.

As the van approached The Rock early that summer morning, I looked across the flat valley to the cliff. From a distance, it looked benign enough. As the van drew nearer, the cliff grew. By the time I was roped in, touching the stone and looking straight up, that cliff was huge.

I had climbed while on my first Outward Bound course the prior fall. Late in the afternoon of that first trip, an instructor suggested I try climbing blind. She must be kidding, I thought, unable to imagine making my way up the cliff without eyes. Her direct look told me she meant it, but she mentioned it only once. Little by little, I grew more curious and mustered the courage to give it a try.

A few people coached me on that first blind climb, up a fairly easy stretch of the cliff. I found their directions confusing. I tuned them out and retreated into myself. Slowly, I reached out to find handholds and slid my foot along the rock, desperately hoping I'd discover small ledges. I felt the stone, warmed by the afternoon sun, and the wind blowing my hair. My knees wouldn't stop shaking. As I reached and pulled, my elbows scraped against the ragged surfaces. Time stood still as I inched my way up the cliff. By the time I made it to the top, I looked as if I'd taken a bad spill off a bicycle. I felt proud and relieved, but realized how unsteady and vulnerable I'd been.

This time, after one easy route, I decided my challenge for the day would be to climb "Pink Lady" blind. Pink Lady, named for the vein of rose quartz that coursed through its center, was the toughest route on the cliff.

Thinking about climbing Pink Lady blind gave me a knot in the pit of my stomach. If I thought about it too much, I'd say forget it. There was no peer pressure. The others on this trip hadn't climbed before. The idea of a blind climb wouldn't occur to them, let alone on Pink Lady. For some reason, I knew I had to do it.

Finally, the Pink Lady route stood empty. I walked over to the rope and tied myself in using the double-eight knot we'd just learned. My knees began to shake as I lifted the bandanna. Then Don, a stranger until that moment, walked up. "Can I help?" He tied the bandanna securely over my eyes.

I rubbed my hands gently across the rock. A few minutes passed. I couldn't stall any longer. "Up rope," I yelled. The person on belay at the top of the cliff pulled the slack out of the climbing rope. I took several deep breaths, trying to steady my knees, and stretched my arms out, tentatively attempting to find that first handhold, knowing that once I took the first step, there was no turning back.

From the beginning of the climb, only Don gave advice. After three or four steps, I realized how competent his coaching was. My legs stopped shaking. My mind calmed. For that time on the cliff, I became one with someone I hardly knew. With his firm, caring voice guiding me on, there was no risk I was afraid to take. I fell into a slow rhythm as he told me where to reach for the next handhold and where to extend my foot for a ledge. The stone came alive through my fingertips. I placed my ear against the granite and listened, hearing the silence of the rock.

Then I got to an overhang near the top of the cliff. My confidence wavered. The dance stopped. I was stuck.

"You're doing great," Don said. "Relax, and feel for the small ledge at your chest. When you have it, push up with both hands with all your might. You'll have to get your knee up to it. There are no footholds."

I tried once and my elbows buckled. I feared I didn't have enough upper-body strength. Then I remembered the thousands of times I'd carried Katherine from her wheelchair to her room and lifted her out of the tub. I had the strength, if I could only find it.

"Susan, concentrate. Give it all you've got."

In one burst of energy, I pushed. My left knee banged against the cliff, scraping back and forth searching for the ledge. I gave one last stretch and grabbed a small handhold, as my badly skinned knee found the narrow ridge. Cheers came from below. I'd made it. The rest was easy.

At the top, I fell into the arms of the guy on belay, overwhelmed with relief and gratitude. After a turn on belay myself, I went down to find Don.

"Great coaching! You'll never know how much you helped me."

"Hey, you did super," he responded. "What a high for me, too."

I sat on my pack at the bottom of the cliff, shaded by scraggly aspens, drinking water from my canteen, feeling exhausted but fulfilled. I took off my safety helmet, leaned back against a boulder, closed my eyes, and felt the dry wind ruffle my hair. Quietly, it dawned on me that I had to be blinded to see.

I drank more water and gobbled a chocolate chip cookie, trying to make sense of that route up Pink Lady. I watched as the others finished their climbs and the instructors gathered the ropes and stuffed them in duffel bags. I didn't move from my boulder.

On the van ride that morning, I'd thought I knew what the day's lessons would be: that people can surpass their own expectations by overcoming self-imposed limits; that strength and accomplishment come from pushing yourself further than you thought possible. I expected the day to hold revelations about individual courage.

Instead, what I took away from that day was less flashy, perhaps more remarkable, in some ways scarier. I hadn't asked for Don's help. I hadn't realized I needed it until I found out how good it felt to have him there, on that cliff with me. Don had no idea what he gave me, how frightened I'd been at first, and how quickly I'd gotten over my fear when I felt safe with him. He stepped up to tie the bandanna without a lot of thought. But once he started, he knew the gravity of the pact.

For the first time, I realized that in those years of struggle with Kat, I'd needed not just an outstretched hand, but the humility to reach back, a mutual gift that requires exposing one's vulnerability and trusting another human being. My strength had been my weakness. I had needed the courage to show my grief. I had needed someone to hold me and hug me as if I were a frightened child, because that is what I had been.

It took me years to understand that the greatest strength comes in knowing when to ask for, and accept, help. Without my forays into the wilderness, I don't know that I ever would have realized that, certainly not so intensely and directly. My wilderness experiences were becoming metaphors for life that stood in full relief. When I needed to, I could flash back to The Rock or that crossing in Baja and relive the lessons. Not only did The Rock teach me the power of an outstretched hand, but it taught me that Mother Nature's arms were continually waiting to welcome me and that they held a healing power.

Sometimes to get to know ourselves, we must push beyond our comfort zones. We must go to the edge of all we have and take one more step.

We skied into Chuck's Place, a backcountry hut reached by a trail that starts at the top of Vail Pass, in a ground blizzard. Our dear friends Wendell and Stephen came with us. Helen and Alice were along for their first cross-country overnight trip. Snow blew so hard, it came down diagonally. Even with my face covered, snow blasted against my cheeks.

Chuck's Place, a cabin made of huge, rough-hewn logs, sits at the top of Shrine Mountain Pass and looks out to the Ten Mile Range, a spectacularly jagged series of peaks.

In the evening, we played poker with M&M's and talked for hours huddled around the woodstove. Wendell and Stephen had patterned Kat for three years. As the evening passed, we reminisced about those years.

"At first, we came for you and Paul," Wendell said. "But that changed. We came for Kat."

"We fell in love with her. We saw the imp in her injured body. She worked so hard for us," Stephen said, shaking his head.

"At first Kat seemed distant and trapped. Over time,

she blossomed. She looked so proud. She always crawled farthest for Stephen," Wendell added. "For some reason, she wanted to please him."

"Hey, she knew what a dashing guy I was. She just wanted to show off," Stephen said, laughing.

"What do you think about when you remember those years?" I asked.

"Kat forced the everyday out of my mind. I know it sounds crazy, but patterning was the single most valuable thing I've done in my adult life." Wendell sat cross-legged on the floor holding a cup of tea to warm her hands.

"What I saw Katherine do in that basement week after week makes climbing Everest look like a jaunt in the park," Stephen said, as tears formed in the corners of his eyes. "I had a unique connection to her. She shared the magic of her perspective with me. I was the privileged one. Katherine touched the injured core in each of us. Time and again, she reached into people's hearts and found that spot. She helped us all build strength from within."

Wendell was pregnant. They had two boys and were hoping for a girl this time. After a lively conversation about the difference between boys and girls, Stephen said, "I hope our little girl is just like Kat." Then he paused, surprised by his own words.

I thought, He's never changed her diapers. He idealizes. He doesn't understand the day in, day out. But I didn't say anything.

Then Stephen looked over at me and corrected himself. "I hope she has Kat's spirit."

If we can only view our lives with a continual sense of discovery . . .

CHAPTER 14

PHOTO BY ALICE PHILLIPS

Susan and Paul, fall 2001.

We move further down the paths of our lives. We allow ourselves to take detours because we are less afraid. We come to trust something deep inside that will tell us what we need to know and what we need to do. Whatever is thrown our way, we can take it into our hearts.

O N A MARCH weekend in 1992, the year after Rita died, we visited Paul Sr. His house seemed empty, but I couldn't put my finger on it. At dinner, it hit. All the children's drawings had been taken down: years' worth of stick-figure family portraits, valentines cut from brightly colored construction paper, cards to Nana and Papa on their fiftieth anniversary. The Ann Landers column with the poem about the Down syndrome child was no longer stuck to the fridge. I walked through the house with a sense still more was missing; then it dawned on me that every picture of Rita had been stored out of sight.

Alice, always observant, saw the blank on the wall above her and asked as she went to bed, "Where's Nana's wedding picture?" A beautiful shot of Rita at twenty in her sweeping satin gown, standing straight, and staring directly at the camera.

I searched the house, looking for signs of Rita, this woman who'd come to mean so much to me and who— when she lay dying, her voice growing weaker each day— had pulled Paul and me to her and whispered, "Celebrate life, children. Celebrate life."

Even pictures where she had been one of a crowd were hidden. I couldn't find the fiftieth wedding anniversary shot of the whole family. I felt as if a porcelain doll had been broken and couldn't be glued back together.

The house had kept Rita vividly alive in my mind. I found comfort glancing at her pictures and seeing her coat hanging in the closet. I had a strange need for the smells of Oil of Olay and Vicks VapoRub that came from the medicine cabinets. I wanted to hold on to all those things that tangibly preserved her memory.

I didn't ask Paul's dad why her images had been removed. No one could fault his loyalty, a husband of fifty years who spent those months in the hospital as she drifted to her death. Perhaps he took down the pictures to begin to forget. Maybe he needed to bury his past to go on with his future.

I woke with apprehension. Paul was away on a business trip. Helen slept at my side. The children rotate when Paul's gone. I needed to get up and begin getting Kat ready for school, but I lay in bed listening to Helen's even breathing.

I moved quietly, grabbing my glasses, a new addition for my over-forty eyes. As I fixed my cup of coffee, I remembered. It was April 23, 1992. Rita had died exactly a year before at 3:00 in the morning. It was 5:00, the time Paul's dad had called with the sad news, which was by then good news. There would be no going back to a grandmother who came laden with packages, Easter baskets, and funny hats.

I sat at the kitchen table and watched the morning light hit the high peaks. I wondered if Paul felt the same sadness in his hotel room in Missouri. I wondered if he remembered.

As she lay dying, Paul Sr. left Rita for a few hours to come up for Easter brunch on our porch. We wore shorts and T-shirts. Lavender pasqueflowers unfurled in our meadow. Daffodils, crocuses, and tulips sprayed color along our deck's edge. Birds sang. No wind blew. I pictured Rita quietly breathing in her small cell, oblivious to one of her favorite days. A week later, she was gone.

The year before, we'd spent Easter at their house in Winter Park. Rita gave all three girls lace dresses and satin hair ribbons. For Mark, she had white pants, a red-and-white-striped shirt, and a navy vest with red sailboats. Rita decorated the house with pastel crepe paper and balloons, stuffed animals, baskets of jelly beans, and Marshmallow Peeps. She wore a broad-brimmed straw hat outlined with plastic daisies. Enough snow had melted for an outdoor hunt. As the eggs were found, we surreptitiously rehid them to prolong the fun.

The Easter after Rita's death, Paul Sr. brought Dottie with him to our house. Dottie, a grade-school classmate from sixty years before, had written when she learned of Rita's death. Paul Sr. asked her to lunch. A romance blossomed.

The children ran to Papa with hugs and kisses. They greeted Dottie with smiles. We hunted Easter eggs as a piercing wind cut through the children's cotton Easter outfits. They put on down jackets and skipped from one egg hiding place to another. Our dog, Freckles—a stray who appeared on our doorstep the day of Rita's funeral—

beat them to a half dozen eggs and slouched guiltily near the front door. Bright red, green, pink, and blue eggshells lay strewn down the front steps. Helen and Alice showed Dottie every picture in their sketchbooks. She showed them pictures of her cats. Kat kept looking around as if she were expecting someone else to arrive.

I sipped my coffee slowly and looked out to the peaks. I remembered all those Easters, knowing certain things could never be the same. I sat, missing Rita and her help in loving Katherine.

Our stories set us free. They are the pollen that floats through the air of our minds, allowing us to reseed. They are the glue, connecting us to people near and far. They are our personal myths, making art of our lives.

Most summers, we visit my parents in New Hampshire. Theirs is a big white clapboard house built in 1833. A porch stretches three-quarters around with daylilies surrounding its base. Dad, as he grew older, strayed from his meager North Dakota upbringing and became a connoisseur of fine wines and antiques. The house is loaded with eighteenth-century American pieces: highboys, lowboys, lots of ball-and-claw feet, Oriental carpets, and sumptuous fabrics.

The yard stretches to a narrow paved road on one side and down a neatly cut hillside with patches of rhododendron and mountain laurel on the other. An old barn attaches to the house at the rear. In it are stored bicycles of every shape and size. No grandchild goes neglected. Badminton and croquet are set up in the side yard under a gigantic evergreen. The old signs of New England surround us: the village green; stone walls; gardens teeming with flowers; giant maple, oak, and birch.

We stroll, run, pick blueberries and raspberries. The kids walk to the candy store and bike around the commons. They mold figures of clay, build bows and arrows out of supple tree branches, play croquet, and organize dress-ups in the attic.

My sister and her brood meet us there. I look forward to the trip while dreading it. It's hard to find moments of uninterrupted time in the midst of perpetual motion. It's hard to keep seven cousins—going seven different directions—happy. My parents' house deteriorates during these visits, its antique charm hidden beneath dirty clothes strewn in every room.

Katherine has never visited. Mother has mentioned she's not sure where Katherine would sleep. I've never pushed it. I've always been able to find a babysitter, and a side of me wants to get away and relax during those summer breaks. There would be no help caring for Kat at my parents'.

Still, not a day passes without pangs. Each year I think how much I wish she were with us—not as the brain-injured child she is, but as a healthy big sister who could play with her cousin Margaret and walk Mark to the candy store. It is a rest to get away, but something is out of whack. The family is not complete. For Katherine to be in a place so perfect, she would need to be perfect, which she never will be, which I can't help her become. Yet I have a feeling she is perfect in her imperfections. Her life is what it was meant to be. There is a beauty in Katherine exactly as she is.

As we head home at the end of our stay, a sadness builds. The next day, I'll change, bathe, and feed Kat. I will, once again, be trapped by her innocence and help-lessness. And I can't wait to get back to her. Without her, there is a hollow in my heart.

Eighty relatives gathered for the family reunion in 1992. We spent a couple of long days in Estes Park at a new lodge with cathedral ceilings, a mammoth stone fireplace, and a large wooden porch looking out to the sheer face of Long's Peak.

Maura danced Irish jigs, her slender legs accented by tight muscles. Heath, a handsome blond, played soccer. I have a black-and-white photo of Kat and these cousins, born within days of her—the three babies lying in a row on our living room's Chinese carpet—when they were a month old.

During the reunion, Mom and Dad never pushed

Kat's wheelchair, never offered to feed or change her, never hugged or spoke to her.

The day after the reunion, I woke in the middle of the night. There were no breezes, no night voices. I felt empty thinking of my children's plane trip the next day. They were heading to my parents' without me. I drank a glass of wine and wrote to fill the void. I awoke early with a deep sense of sorrow. Slowly I understood: I mourned the loss of my parents. I wondered if they knew how far from them I felt.

To cope with Kat, I have sought out those people like Rita and Linda Orona, who loved Katherine as she was and took comfort from her. Those who held her close and looked directly in her eyes. Those who felt no embarrassment, but understood the peace of her presence. My parents couldn't see beyond Katherine's crooked body. Every time they visited and left without a word for Katherine, the wall in my heart grew higher.

A friend, a therapist who happens to call at my most desperate moments, says, "Reach out a hand and help take them step-by-step with an open heart. They are frightened. They don't understand. Can you be that generous?"

I don't know. The core is still raw and the journey has been lonely. I'm not sure they can join the path this far down the road. I'm not sure I can go back and quietly, patiently lead them down the path that I so feared and fought against.

———

We journey back, searching for something we had in child-
hood—a freshness, an innocence, an ability to live fully and
completely right now. If we keep going on this route, we
retrieve our laughter.

I found myself seeking out wilderness adventures. They
provided an escape, but also an intensity that made me
feel completely alive. The alchemy of healing is mysteri-
ous, but I had no doubt that my relationship with nature
was key to my getting better, not bitter. Soon after that
family reunion in July 1992, we had the opportunity to go
on an Outward Bound rafting course and we took it.

We began at the mythic Gates of Lodore Canyon in
northeastern Utah and wound down the Green River into
Colorado, following John Wesley Powell's path through
rapids with names like Disaster Falls and Hell's Half Mile.
Solo time came. My home for the night was a quiet beach
at the base of a steep red-rocked canyon in Dinosaur
National Monument. I was alone with my sleeping bag,
water bottle, and hairbrush.

When I signed on for this raft trip with educators
from around the country, I didn't realize the route it
would take. If I had known, I might have hesitated. I
might have decided there were other courses that would
challenge me but wouldn't force the same confrontation

with my past. The second day on the river, with a flash of comprehension, I realized where we were.

Twelve years ago, we took Kat on her first camping trip. Now we rafted by the place: Echo Park, a vast amphitheater where the canyons of the Green and Yampa rivers converge. A mile above the junction, our boat crew stopped paddling. We lay on our backs on the raft's thick gray tubing, floating quietly through the calm section of the river. We wound under the shadow of Steamboat Rock, seven hundred feet straight up. The golden gray of the gracefully curved rock soared over us, precariously balanced, looking as if it would tip and crush us at any minute. No one spoke. We closed our eyes and felt the boat's smooth flow. We floated through the air, a magic carpet on the back of the desert wind.

Then we came to the spot. I saw where we had parked the car, pitched our tent, begun our hike with Kat snuggled deep in the backpack. That weekend in 1980, we drove all day to Echo Park to camp. Our friends brought a tent big enough to stand in. We huddled inside talking, laughing, eating. Luke and Rosa fixed beef Stroganoff. Wine flowed. Spirits soared. Outside the wind howled. Kat sat in the midst of us all, a chubby, smiling nine-month-old, the center of attention. Back in our tent, I wrapped my down sleeping bag around us, a soft cocoon binding us forever as the zipper closed. I drifted in and out of sleep as I held Kat at the gentle curve of my waist and bent knees.

The next morning it snowed. I remember watching a boatload of wet, bedraggled people float by on a raft. We dressed Kat in a snowsuit and mittens. As we hiked, soft flakes landed on her nose. She giggled and opened her mouth to catch the snow on her tongue. We traipsed up trails searching for petroglyphs and broad views over the dry gorges.

I hadn't thought of Kat's first camping trip for years. As we drifted down the river closer to the spot, I felt her presence. She hasn't changed much. She's just bigger and thinner. She couldn't walk or talk then, either.

Helen, Alice, and Mark went back to New Hampshire with my parents after the family reunion. The night before Paul and I left for the raft trip, I lay on Kat's bed snuggling her in my arms. I curled my legs next to hers and wrapped my arms around her waist. "We're going away for a few days. Helen, Alice, and Mark are visiting Mimi. Kelly will take care of you. We'll all be back soon. We love you, Kat. We'll always be here for you."

When I looked at her face, one tear flowed down her soft cheek.

I was designated to captain our boat, *The Artful Dodger*, through Hell's Half Mile. Huge boulders littered the river, creating foaming bursts of water. On my first white-water raft trip, I didn't know what I was doing. I forced a look of calm to hide the queasiness in my stomach.

Sitting at the back of *The Artful Dodger*, I used my paddle to guide our raft through the wild waters. We made it down in several seconds. I couldn't remember the route we'd taken or how we'd made it through safely. All the tension drained out of my body when I looked back and saw the crocodile's teeth of boulders we'd slipped through. We patted ourselves on our backs, bragging about *The Artful Dodger*'s prowess in the rapids and basking idly in our accomplishment.

We had left the worst of Hell's Half Mile behind when the *Dodger* hit a sleeper, a large rock buried just beneath the surface of the rushing water, hard. I bounced up like a jack-in-the-box. The boat swept forward. I found myself out of the boat, clinging to a sharp rock in churning water that thrust against my legs, pushing me into the cauldron of white foam and boulders. I grabbed the safety rope on the side of the raft as the Outward Bound instructor clutched my arm, pulling me back in the boat. Back in the safety of *The Artful Dodger*, I remembered I'd had the same fleeting terror on the final crossing in Baja and on the ledge near the top of Pink Lady. I wanted to grab those moments, to push my limits and find that edge where I felt totally alive. But I also knew neither Hell's Half Mile nor Pink Lady had taught me half as much as Kat's lone tear.

I carefully positioned my sleeping bag on the rocky slope to have a broad view of the river and canyon wall. I sat on my bag, pulled my knees to my chest, wrapped my arms around my legs, and took sips from my water bottle. The sky lay silver to the west as the last light of day faded. The canyon's depth hid the colors of the sunset. The evening star hung above the canyon's rim. Cicadas chirped. The river rushed by. I sat weeping, remembering.

In the middle of solo night, I awoke stunned by the thick blanket of stars over me. A shooting star lit up the eastern sky, brilliant, wild, then gone so fast I wondered if I'd seen anything at all. A stoic satellite moved on its silent journey. When I opened my eyes again, the morning light struck the sheer canyon walls and an eagle soared overhead, a lone sentry in an immense, empty land. I lay listening to the river, drifting in and out of sleep, no longer saddened by thoughts of the past.

Then I looked up at the cliff and saw it: a face old, wizened, and wrinkled. A face carved in the rock by wind and water that captured the wisdom of the ages in its craggy cheekbones, bushy eyebrows, and shock of curly hair. Several times I looked away, thinking I must be imagining things. Each time, my eyes came back to its crooked lips and deep-set eyes.

It spoke slowly, a word a minute, a word an hour, a word a year. It held me under its spell. It was as if no time had passed between the camping trip years before with Katherine and this quiet morning on the banks of the Green River. Our lives passed as quickly as the rushing water through Hell's Half Mile. I stared at its roughly chiseled features, our conversation weighted by the millions of years the face had looked out from its rocky roost.

In the canyons, there are many faces on cliff walls. Faces that have watched the breathing of rocks and rivers for millions of years. Faces that have looked on mute, as the rivers carved and the hawks soared. How can it be that Katherine has one of those faces?

CHAPTER 15

Katherine, Susan, Alice, Paul, Helen, and Mark, summer 1992.

There are loud voices in each of us we don't listen to: voices that haunt us in our dreams and taunt us in our waking hours. When we have lost something precious, when our hopes have been dashed, we listen more to those voices. As we seek our way, we listen to voices we've spent our lives silencing. When we listen very carefully, the clamor turns to quiet and the quiet to song.

AFTER THE Green River, my life felt like a series of rapids. Work no longer satisfied me. I awakened daily with my stomach tied in knots. Many mornings I lay in bed, unable to shake the image of the rocky face in the canyon wall. I sensed it held answers for me if I would just listen.

A couple of weeks after returning from the raft trip, I spent a hot July day at a conference. Midafternoon, an emptiness crept into my heart, dissolving my ability to concentrate. I left early with a gnawing sense I had something to do.

Years before, we had tried to potty train Katherine. For months, she had success on a small potty chair with a flimsy plastic tray. We sat by her on the kitchen's linoleum floor, feeding her as she sat. She grew. Her legs stretched too far. She fell off the potty chair, unable to keep her balance.

Paul bought her a simple wooden high chair. Carefully, he sawed a hole in the middle of its seat, sanded it smooth, shellacked it shiny. He attached ridges to its bottom and found a plastic bowl that worked as the potty. Kat sat proudly on her specially designed seat. We cheered her, praised her, patted her.

Little by little, she lost interest. We couldn't find her rhythm. We became discouraged by the failures. Silently, we agreed it didn't matter. Diapers were no big deal.

We bought another high chair and stored the potty high chair in the garage with cast-off bicycles, toys, and furniture. The replacement high chair broke. We resurrected the high chair potty, wiping off the thick film of dirt. Every time we fed Kat, the chair left creases on her bottom where Paul had crafted the hole.

The impermanence of the by then decrepit potty brought a particular sadness. Too many of our hopes were reflected in it. I had to look away every time I fed Kat.

On the way home from the conference that July day, I stopped at several discount stores. They carried only high chairs with wide plastic trays and vinyl seats with teddy bear, choo-choo train, or doll baby patterns. I wanted sturdiness—a solid chair that brought Kat pleasure and gave me comfort.

I walked into a small furniture store filled with cribs, swinging chairs, chests of drawers, stuffed animals, high chairs, and car seats. Then, across the room, I saw its pale wood and solid frame. My eyes made their way through the chaos of merchandise to where it sat near the cash register, waiting with its gently curved back, strong legs, and sculpted seat.

I rubbed my hand along its smooth seat and sat in it, trying out its contours. I tied the safety belt carefully around my waist, checking to make sure it would fit Kat as she grew. It cost twice as much as the other chairs in the store. I justified the expense. This was the mountain bike Katherine would never have. I imagined how it would feel to her as she grew bigger and older.

I loaded the huge box in the back of my car. On the drive home, the gnawing left and a silly smile swallowed my face. That day, I'd done exactly what I'd wished to do. I had begun to listen to the face in the canyon wall.

At home I screwed the pieces together, then carried Katherine into the kitchen and set her firmly on the throne, latching the heavy tray across the chair's arms.

"It's beautiful, Kat," I said. "I got it so we'll always have a sturdy seat just for you."

She grinned and beat one arm against the other, as if she were clapping. I ruffled her hair, gave her a big hug, and stroked the curved back of the high chair. This one we'd never have to throw away.

What is it that sets us free? What is it that gives us the strength to be ourselves? Is it our ability to love, with no strings attached? Is it love that will save us?

The power of the Green River stayed with me—the sound of the water and the wind alive in my head. I needed time to slow down so I could hear it from deep inside.

The urge to move on had taken hold. Each day I left the house knowing the passion I'd once had for my work had dimmed, thinking about the words of Kenny Rogers's song "The Gambler": "You got to know when to hold 'em, know when to fold 'em."

I arranged a six-week leave of absence—a chance to take care of minor surgery, test a less-hectic life, and write more about Katherine. We had a cockeyed garage twenty paces from our front door renovated into a writing room. I thought a six-week break would be just what I needed to finish Kat's story and then hop back in the fray.

My leave began on my forty-first birthday. It was also Katherine's birthday week. Paul had two business trips. Our babysitter was on her honeymoon. It was the first time I had taken care of all four children alone for a week.

I feared the time with Katherine, afraid I'd be unable to bear the strain of caring for her by myself. Each afternoon I'd wheel Katherine in from her bus, feed her dinner, then sit in the library and hold her in my arms. At first she'd wring her hands. Then she'd stop and become calm and still. Together, we looked out to the Continental Divide.

It took me all those years to get to that point of peace with Katherine, to hold her and ask nothing more of her, to hear her silent speech and love her for it. With Katherine, there were many things I thought I could never do. Over the years, little by little, I did them. Mainly, I kept her with us in her flowered room. Slowly, Katherine moved from the rim of my heart to its quiet center.

The needle went deep in my spine. I sat on the operating table hugging a pillow. Two anesthesiologists stood over my hunched form.

"She's all crooked. Hold her shoulders so she'll stay straight."

I jumped as I felt the needle poking around again, then curved my back more, hoping they'd find the spot and leave me alone. I took two deep breaths and held perfectly still.

"I've got it!" said the doctor with the needle.

They rotated me onto the table—the needle in my spine already starting its job of numbing my lower body. The only other time I'd had an epidural was when Katherine was born.

A hodgepodge of voices surrounded me. I lay on the operating table wondering why I'd arranged the surgery the second week of my leave. I didn't want to dredge up the hospital memories from those early, desperate days with Katherine, but I could feel them coming.

In the glass front of a medicine cabinet, I saw the reflection of my leg swabbed with bright orange Mercurochrome. I drifted into a drugged sleep as they freed my left leg of the thick dark lines that had throbbed through it since I was pregnant with Alice.

Varicose veins, the sign my body wasn't what it used to be: veins that hurt on hikes and runs and made me self-conscious in shorts and bathing suits. I was happy to get rid of them, but no one had told me about the catheter in my back, the nausea after surgery, the teeth chattering and body shaking.

Twelve years before, we took Kat to the same hospital

for diagnostic tests. They took vial after vial of blood and did two spinal taps. We laid Kat on her side and curved her body into a fetal position. I leaned over her like a giant spider, holding her head and her knees so she wouldn't move. She screamed until I thought my eardrums would shatter. The doctors assured me it didn't hurt.

As I lay there, the same sense of loss I'd felt as we floated by Echo Park overwhelmed me. Again, when I least expected it, I was brought face-to-face with images from my life with Katherine—images I thought I'd handled years ago.

The weekend before surgery, we had a major clearing out of junk. Into the center of the basement playroom we emptied all the wicker baskets and items from the toy closet. It was easy to toss the extra dolls and stuffed animals, most of them beyond repair. We attacked the mess, my sense of accomplishment growing with each toy placed in the giveaway pile. Then, in the midst of the confusion, I saw Kat's activity center, still brightly colored and in good shape. Mark rushed to it and twirled its knobs and batted its levers. I sat, unable to move, and remembered the day I unscrewed it from Katherine's crib and buried it in the back of her closet. It passed down to the other children, but none of them loved it as Katherine had.

I let Mark play with it for a while, then reminded him of the work at hand. He moved on to the plastic cars and train set. Helen asked, "What's wrong, Mom?" sensing my quiet loneliness.

"Nothing," I said, picking up the activity center. "What do you think about this?" I held it up to show her.

"It's for a little baby, Mom. We don't need it."

I hugged the activity center to my chest and held in my mind the picture of Katherine sitting in her crib, oblivious to what had been her favorite toy. I hesitated a moment before stuffing it into the Goodwill bag.

Those images found me as I lay on the operating table, drifting to unconsciousness. I knew for the rest of my life those memories would continue to rise randomly to the surface of my mind.

Mine was day surgery. Early in the afternoon, a nurse helped me into a wheelchair to take me down to the car. "How are you doing?" she asked.

"I'm fine except for the grogginess and the nausea."

She handed me a plastic bowl. In the elevator, I began hiccuping. One cough came up from the bottom of my gut and filled the bowl with vomit. The nurse wiped my forehead with a wet washcloth and wheeled me into a restroom as the other people in the corridor stared. I dumped the vomit in the toilet and flushed it away.

Heavy stainless-steel equipment rolled down the halls. People ran around in baggy green suits. The image of Rita lying in the bed at Fitzsimmons Hospital weeks before her death shot through my mind. The heavy scent of Pine-Sol covered the smells of pain and sorrow.

I wanted to leave the pale walls and catheters behind. I wanted to stretch out in my own bed, bury myself in my down comforter, and never think of hospitals again.

How do we let go of our guilt? How do we get to the point of saying we did what we did and now we must let go of that past and embrace what we are now, what we have become because of our sorrow?

The first fall storm brought a foot of heavy snow, breaking branches and smothering the last summer flowers. Several days later, temperatures had crept back to the sixties. Kat's bus brought her home at 2:45. The Indian summer breeze warmed my face as I wheeled her in. On the spur of the moment, I decided to stroll Kat to pick up Mark at preschool.

From our house the dirt road is flat and begins to slope gently downhill. I ran with Kat over this section. She threw back her head, a look of terror on her face, then burst out laughing on the downward grade. I kept running. My leg—three weeks after the operation—felt strong as I panted past the picnic grounds, checking my watch every few minutes, wondering if we could make it in time.

The curving hill that rises steeply from the picnic

grounds was full of ruts and puddles from the melting snow. I got stuck in the mud and had to lift the front wheels from the muck before pushing her forward. We'll never make it, I thought. What am I trying to prove anyway? I kept on, my heart pounding as I pushed the heavy wheelchair up the hill.

From the top of the hill, it's downhill. We wouldn't be very late. Kat and I began a sprint to the finish.

Another mother opened the door for me. I parked Kat in the hall and headed downstairs to get Mark. Mark threw his arms around my legs and said, "Wow, Mom, you brought Kat!" as we climbed the steps.

We rushed across the road to the girls' school. Kat sat, sucking her thumb.

When Alice came out, she asked a couple of friends if they'd like to meet Katherine. They had studied Helen Keller earlier in the year. Alice had told the whole class about Kat. The third graders circled around. Alice asked her friends, "Isn't she pretty?" They nodded. By then, kids poured out. When they passed Kat they stared, surprised to see someone in a wheelchair on their playground.

We found Helen. The five of us walked home together, no hurry now. Helen shared the day's high points. Mark took the shortcut down the sledding hill, sliding all the way. Kat smiled. It was the first time I'd taken Kat to the other children's schools. I felt the same sense of pride as when I crossed the finish line in my first marathon, years before.

My feet killed me. My knees ached. I didn't want Paul to cheer me up. I had every reason to be a grump. Each downhill step felt like knives in my kneecaps.

Maybe I'd overdone it climbing Mount of the Holy Cross, a majestic fourteen-thousand-foot peak in Colorado's Sawatch Range, a month after leg surgery. It was the last weekend of my leave before going back to work. Early that morning, Paul and I had stood on the balcony at the Eagle River Inn, where we'd spent the night so we could get an early start. We'd watched the bright stars and the coming of dawn in the crystal clear sky and knew it would be a perfect day for the ascent.

On the east face of this climb, ragged granite forms the arms of a cross. Much of the year, a giant snow crucifix spreads majestically below the jagged peak. A huge boulder field reaches to the top of Holy Cross. For a thousand vertical feet, it's a scramble from rock to rock. We struggled up, committed to making the summit on our last hike of the season.

At the top we stretched out on boulders, basking in the warm sun as we ate our sandwiches and looked out to waves of peaks, flowing in every direction. On that windless, clear day, we rested at the top of the mountain, for a flicker of time living the life of an eagle soaring above the earth.

After the elation of the summit, my body gave out on the downhill. The fifty-four hundred vertical feet of downward pounding brought tears to my eyes. My toes and knees had had it. At first my spirits held. Then I grew silent, disgruntled about my physical discomfort, until a ten-year-old image of Katherine, crawling back and forth on our basement's red concrete floor, with her small jaw set in determination, butted its way into my mind and kept me going.

Hiking for nine hours cleared the cobwebs from my head. Trudging through the pine forest, down by the fast-moving stream, and across the boulder field had brought focus to my thoughts. I knew I had to leave my job. On that climb, I heard the message I'd avoided for months. I had to follow the path I'd begun that warm spring day in Taos. I had to devote more of myself to Kat.

My short leave had shown me the power and beauty of solitude, something that had frightened me all my life. Katherine's lone tear before we left for the raft trip had been too eloquent to ignore. I had begun to feel at peace with her. Finally, I could enter her room with a sense of joy rather than sadness. Finally, I could look into her large gray eyes and have a sense of the messages from her soul without being sidetracked into despair by the contortions of her crippled body. That day I knew I would quit my job, say no to boards and committees, and simplify my life so that I could hear what Katherine had to teach me. A loud voice badgered me to step back so I could take the inner journey. Kat had forced me to peer inside. I'd been a human doing; maybe if I listened to Kat's messages well enough, I could become a human being.

We must go to those places of pain that sit at our core like molten lava. There, we are burned to ash. All that came before has changed. The pain and fire have become a part of us. The ash becomes fertilizer for new growth.

CHAPTER 16

Alice, Mark, and Helen, 1992.

OUR BOAT

Life got rough
as it tends to
The quilts got threadbare
and we forgot everything
But our small boat
tossing in the waves
Burden or savior

We didn't guess
Yet here we are to tell our tale
and laugh over our despair.

I WAS on a trip the day they celebrated Halloween at school. Helen and Alice made Katherine's costume.

"Mom, I thought the best way was to start with solid colors and build from there," Helen said matter-of-factly, describing the black stirrup pants and black turtleneck they'd used for Katherine's cat outfit. "We taped cardboard ears to a red hair band and made a brown felt tail that we sewed to a black belt."

Mark butted in, "Hey, Mom, I colored the ears."

Her sisters painted black whiskers on Kat's cheeks and sent extra face paints to Margaret Walters School for a touch-up later in the day. Helen wrote a note to Kat's teacher explaining everything.

"Mom, you should have seen Kat's face. She looked awesome," Alice added.

"Charge!" Mark yelled that evening as the children scrambled out of the van and ran toward the house, yelling, "Trick or treat." Alice led the way, always first to the door, then bounded back to the van, taking the seat closest to the door. The others filed in. A salting of snow covered the ground and soft flakes fell. Mud puddles had turned to ice.

Mark wore a gray plastic knight's outfit, complete with sword. At every house he fell on the ice. Warnings to slow down reached deaf ears. He was drawn into the magic of All Hallows' Eve and could only run. After each splat, he pulled himself up and pushed to the front of the gang of kids.

Several days before, Mark had come into my room. "Mom, I'm afraid Kat had a nightmare."

"How do you know, Mark?"

"I went into her room and she was tossing around."

"Is she okay now?"

"Yeah, I took care of her. I patted her head and whispered, 'It's okay, Kataloo,' and she calmed right down."

I went with them to a few houses and then headed home to be with Kat. She lay buried beneath her flowered comforter in her small, warm room. She reminded me of Rita that last Easter when she lay dying, missing her favorite holiday.

I stretched out next to her on her bed, thinking of the Halloweens that had passed her by. When Mary, our babysitter during the patterning days, had lived with us, she made elaborate Halloween costumes for the children. She scoured Goodwill stores and fabric shops. Months in advance, she pulled out her sewing machine. Scraps littered her small apartment—sequins, organdy, feathers, glitter. Always, she made the most beautiful costume for Katherine.

One year Kat was a ballerina dressed in Chinese slippers, white tights, and a brilliant red tutu. The next year, she was a princess dressed in pink from her glittering crown to her ballet shoes. The last year Mary was with us, she created a clown costume with a cone hat attached to wild yarn hair and sewed ruffled sleeves and a collar to a red blanket sleeper. Kat went with the others on those first Halloweens. As she grew bigger, it became harder.

I stroked Kat's cheek until the doorbell rang. A hamburger and giant fries stood on the porch, crying, "Trick or treat." They grabbed M&M's and miniature Heath bars from the basket and ran from the house into the darkness. I went back to Kat's room, dimmed the lights, folded her cat outfit, and stored it on the shelf in her closet next to the clown costume from Mary.

When Rita lived, she played Santa. Often, the dresses she bought were too big or too gaudy. But the girls always donned them with delight and danced through the house in ruffles and velvet. Kat was not forgotten. We dressed her in tights, one of Rita's frilly dresses, and patent leather shoes.

On the day before Christmas the year after Rita's death, I went into Kat's room to strip off her stale clothes. As I bent down to her, she gave me that look: head tipped down, eyes up, mouth in a slight grin. She held her thin hands together as if she were praying. I talked to her about

Christmas as I pulled off her stirrup pants and wiped her bottom clean.

Then the gnawing began. What was she trying to tell me? Why couldn't she blurt it out, just this once? I had bought new sheets, several colorful sweat suits, air freshener, and hair bows for her. What was missing? The others express their wants and needs daily. I never have to guess what's on their Christmas lists.

On the way to the ice skating lake, the gnawing grew. I asked Paul to stop at a clothing store. "It'll just take a minute." I went immediately to the dress rack with Helen and Alice and began rifling through the Christmas finery.

When I was thirteen my mother took me to a small boutique near Woodsfield, Ohio, to buy a Christmas dress. We found the plainest gray wool with long sleeves, white cuffs and collar, and a small maroon bow at the neck. When I think of my adolescence, that is the dress I remember. Perhaps Kat remembered her dresses from Rita, too.

Helen and Alice pulled out dresses one at a time. We narrowed it to two. One was prettier and cost twice as much. The other would do. At the checkout, the salesgirl mentioned that the other dress was on sale. I rushed back and picked it off the rack, wondering how many years it might fit Katherine, a child's size 10 for my thirteen-year-old. I folded it carefully——a Heidi dress with a wide red skirt, small blue and green flowers in vertical stripes, and long sleeves that buttoned at the cuff—and laid it gently in the bag.

"You don't need to wrap it," I said, wanting to be able to admire it when I got home.

"I found just what I was looking for," I told Paul as I jumped into the front seat. I held the bag on my lap as if it were a new baby until tears streamed down my cheeks.

"I don't know why it makes me sad. She deserves this. She'll look so pretty when we take her to Christmas dinner."

Paul glanced my way and said gently, "It'll make her Christmas. Kat'll love it." He paused. "And now that Mom's dead, if not you, who?"

> *My sister is very loving*
> *But her brain is damaged.*
> *Is there any way*
> *You could help me help her?*
> *Her name is Katherine*
> *My mother worked on her many years*
> *Before I was even thought of.*
> *Do remember, please help me and her.*
>
> ALICE, AGE 7

Christmas night, Alice strokes Kat's head as it rests against her shoulder. Together they sit on the sofa covered by a sleeping bag, watching *The Sound of Music*.

Ever since she was a baby, Alice patted Kat and played with her. As she grew older, she wanted to sleep with Kat on Kat's double-bed mattress on the floor. She massages Kat's feet when they're blue and cold. She doesn't pity Kat or analyze the situation. To Alice, Kat is Kat. She loves her as she is. She has never told me she wishes Kat were able to be a big sister. They are soul mates in a way I don't understand.

Soon Katherine sleeps. Alice continues to caress her hair. I carry Kat to bed and lay her in the middle of her new sheets, still stiff and creased at the folds. She opens her eyes briefly, smiles, then drifts peacefully into her Christmas night's dreams.

The day before, Alice scoured the house for fabric. She found red cotton with small white hearts and a bag of cotton balls, then closed the door to the guest room.

Hours later, she came out with a small pillow raised in her hands like an offering to a queen. "Mom, do you think Kat'll like it? It'll be soft for her head."

Helen made a doll for Kat. She cut its form from white cloth, stuffed it, sewed its sides, and painted its face with Magic Markers. "It's the thought that counts, Mom," she said proudly, as she hung the doll on the doorknob of Kat's small closet.

I snuggled beside Alice in her flannel sheets. She wrapped a short sturdy leg around my knees and we began our nightly game. "Alice, what are you thinking right now?"

"I was thinking about Katherine."

"What were you thinking about her?"

"I was thinking whoever made Kat put her into our family because he knew we could handle it. He knew we needed Kat, that she'd be a great part of our lives."

"What d'ya mean, Ali?" I ask.

"He knew we had it in us to keep her at home and love her. Some families wouldn't love her. If he gave Kat to a family who didn't love her, she'd be abused. She's different, Mom, and she needs a loving family to take care of her."

I lay scratching her back, wondering where she had found the words she spoke.

"Mom, Kat's like a god to us. She brings so much into our lives. She's made for us. She couldn't be anybody else's. If we didn't have Katherine, we wouldn't have such important lives."

"But Alice, it isn't always easy for you, is it?"

"Well, Kat makes the mornings a real hassle. It's hard because we're so busy and we have six people in our family and Kat is always the first thing on the agenda. It's hard having a sister like that . . . but wonderful in a way."

A couple of years before, also around the Christmas holidays, I'd rushed down to ride my stationary bicycle early in the morning. I was, as usual, behind before the day began. I grabbed Helen's third-grade folder. At least I could review her week's work as I pedaled. Midway

through the stack of papers, this little poem, full of mis-
spellings, dropped to the floor.

> *I am dreaming of my sister.*
> *I am dreaming because she is hurt.*
> *I do not think she will ever be well again.*
> *My sister is brain damaged,*
> *But still I am hoping every day*
> * she will be all right.*
> *I am dreaming that for Christmas*
> * something will happen*
> * so she is a normal child.*
> *Anything can happen*
> * It can be magic dust,*
> * or special words.*
> *And, I guess you can say*
> * I want a miracle.*

I sat on my bike seat completely still and read the
poem again and again. At breakfast, I asked Helen why
she had written the poem.

"Our teacher asked us to write about what we wanted
for Christmas. Lots of kids wanted games. One boy
wanted his cousin home safe from the Gulf War. Cyndi
wanted world peace. That was what I wanted."

"Helen, what's it like for you having Kat for a sister?
Be honest . . . you won't hurt my feelings."

"Katherine's always been here, Mom. I've never
known anything else. I love her."

"But do you feel sad you don't have a big sister?"

"Oh, I get mad and sad that Kat can't pave the way, do things first, tell me about them. Sometimes it's hard being the first kid to do things, but she's given us so much."

"Like what?"

"If I miss five on my spelling test, I tell myself to think about Kat. When kids in the class are mean to each other or say mean things about a handicapped person, I think of Kat and know they don't understand."

"You don't feel Kat slows us down, keeps us from doing things as a family?"

Helen put her hands on her hips and sighed, "Mom, tell me one way Kat has slowed us down. Kat brought us together. We have more love in our lives. We still go on raft trips, to Chuck's Place, to New Hampshire, Taos, hiking, picnics. She's never slowed us down. This is a hard family to stop."

Yet, one day before we left for a vacation, I'd walked into Kat's room and found Helen awkwardly holding Kat, rocking her back and forth, with tears running down her cheeks to the top of Kat's head.

"Why are you so sad?" I'd asked.

"It breaks my heart to see Kat alone in her room when all of us are hustling and bustling to leave her. It makes me so sad to think she'll be here with a babysitter when we're all off having fun."

I remembered that time as Helen said, "Don't you get it, Mom? Kat keeps us from just living on the surface."

A two-year-old came up to Katherine and touched her cheek, saying, "She baby." She patted Katherine's back, then hopped on the rocking horse. Katherine slept on the nursery's carpeted floor.

The nursery at Loveland Basin, a family ski area low on glitz, welcomes Katherine. Loveland is set high above the tree line, reaching almost to the Continental Divide. It rises above Eisenhower Tunnel, the east-west connection that bores through a mountain to get skiers to their destinations more quickly.

The nursery is up a small hill from the parking lot. Paul hurt his back last summer so I've been lifting Kat more. Kat weighs 65 pounds. I weigh 110. I'm not sure how much longer I'll be able to tote her around.

Holiday traffic slowed us down and we arrived late to Loveland. We couldn't park as close as usual. I held Kat tightly in my arms, locked my fingers together under her bottom, and carried her to the nursery.

"Great, it's Katherine," Beverly greeted her with a big hug. "I didn't think you were coming today, Kat."

I propped her in an overstuffed chair in front of the TV as Beverly got a plaid blanket to wrap around her shoulders. She swayed to Raffi videos in her front-row seat.

At noon, we came back to the nursery to change Kat and feed her lunch: a banana and a peanut butter and jelly sandwich moistened with juice. I leaned her back against the front of the big chair and covered her with a towel, then knelt beside her feeding her each bite. After lunch, I laid her on the floor to sleep.

By the end of the day, carrying Kat to the car was tough. I slipped twice and felt as if my arms were being yanked out of their sockets. Helen rushed to open the car door. I put Kat's long, bony legs in first, then rotated her body into the seat, banging her head and mine.

Paul never cries at movies. He never cries period. He bundles his feelings inside. In all the years with Kat, I can't remember tears.

But Paul cried when we watched *Awakenings*. Profoundly retarded patients, all of whom had suffered from encephalitis—"sleeping sickness"—during an epidemic in the 1920s, are brought out of their trance by the "miracle drug" L-dopa. Leonard awakens from a sleep of thirty years. He is brought out of his deep freeze a handsome, charming man full of spirit.

Then the dopamine backfires. Leonard develops a twitch that begins in his neck and spreads quickly. He loses control of his body and shakes all over. He is like a bug before the final kill—twitching, kicking, trying to gain control, but ultimately becoming lifeless.

Leonard knows what's happening but has no power to reverse the ravages of the disease or the false hope of the drug. He becomes belligerent and angry. Toward the end, there is a scene of Leonard in bed as his mother pins on his diaper. He seems as if there had been no awakening.

During *Awakenings,* Helen looked up at me gravely and said, "Mom, I'd want Kat to be awakened. Then I could get to know her, then I could understand. It would be worth it, even if for a short time."

Even now I keep hoping, though not believing, that there might be a miracle drug for Kat. But the miracle might, like Leonard's, be a hoax, a bitter interlude. Maybe that thought brought Paul's tears.

When I was young, a robin flew into the picture window at the back of our house and fell stunned to the ground. We gathered around, fearing it had died, killed by the window's deception. We picked it up and placed it carefully in a shoe box lined with cotton balls. It lay peaceful, quiet, protected, until several hours later it flew away.

Paul treated Katherine like the robin. He created a soft, protected world for her. He fed and changed her. He carried her to her bed and stroked her crooked back. He served Katherine day in, day out.

In many ways he did a better job than I. He fit her quietly into his routine. She was always his little

Katherine. On some level, I think he knew his steady response to her was the only way he could help me.

For years we didn't talk about Katherine much. When we did, Paul looked like a child watching a truck run over his first bicycle. I couldn't stand to look him in the eye.

My memories of Paul from that early time are blurry. We walked parallel tracks, side by side, but not touching. Much later I asked him why those years are surrounded in fog.

"God, Sue, it was like we were on a sinking ship, each trying to put out fires and throw buckets of water overboard. We didn't have much time for each other. Kat's problems permeated everything and then with the other kids. . . . That doesn't mean I didn't love you. I always loved you."

Many days I wanted to flee. I didn't know the value of sticking together and muddling through. It took going to the brink to come back and rebuild. Little by little, we fell in love in a new way. If our lives had flowed smoothly by, we might have grown bored. It took years to appreciate Paul's willingness to quietly stand by me and Katherine. I hadn't known the parallel paths would finally cross.

Alice drew a brightly colored picture of two teddy bears, one yellow and one brown, floating in a green sky holding hearts. An apple and a basket are suspended in the thick crayon strokes near the bears. It was a picture full of fantasy. Alice begged to hang it in Kat's room. "Her room's boring, Mom. She needs it."

Together, Alice and I trimmed the picture and framed it. Alice pulled out the Windex, wiping all the fingerprints off the glass and rubbing the brass frame until you could see your reflection.

As Kat knelt on her bed, Alice displayed the picture proudly before her and told her about the bears, "They'll keep you company when you're alone in here, Kat. I hope you like it." Alice hugged Kat, then ran outside to play.

I propped the picture against the wall in Kat's room. I didn't think to be careful or worry that she might hit it. She never gets out on that side. But that night, she rolled out of bed on the wrong side. The next morning, I opened her door. At first I didn't see her. Then I realized she was lying next to Alice's gift, staring at the yellow bear.

> *My Rose, my cross*
> *I will bleed and carry you*
> *Everywhere they shall see you*
> *And when they say they love you*
> *I'll weep like grateful rain*
> *And when they forget you*
> *I will scream your name*

HELEN, AGE 11

CHAPTER 17

PHOTO BY K. L. TARTAKOFF

Mark, Alice, Susan, Katherine, Paul, and Helen, 1999.

If we can look at our lives as adventures, if we understand at the outset that on an adventure nothing is certain and there are no guarantees, if we can persevere through the Arctic winds and desert heat, if we can move forward with our eyes and hearts open, if we can accept whatever is thrown our way, our lives become a beautiful song in a minor key.

I HAVE written Katherine's eulogy a hundred times in my mind. There have been days of high fevers and seizures when I thought she couldn't make it much longer. Women with Rett syndrome can live for decades, but there is a period between the ages of five and fourteen when a puzzling form of sudden death can occur in sleep.

When Katherine is sick, I feel a closer bond. Drawn by her helplessness and fragility, I open my heart. She brings out a tenderness I didn't know existed beneath my tough exterior.

I see myself at her funeral, a small affair with a circle of close friends, and wonder if I'll have the presence of mind to paint a vignette of her life. I'll give it my best. I owe Katherine that.

I often wonder why it took me so long to accept Katherine. My journey with her has been clumsy and halting. I walked in mud—stuck time and again. Her beauty was too mixed with confusion and pain. I saw something on the other side of the pain, but I didn't know how to get there.

For a year after I left work, I took care of Kat alone. Paul helped with breakfast, but I dressed her, bathed her, fed her, changed her, day after day. I'm not sure why I needed to care for Kat so completely. I think I was doing penance. I was asking her for forgiveness. I had to get very close to be able to hear her. It took holding her, slowing down, spending hours alone in my small writing room, allowing the images from her life to spill forth, for me to get to the point where I could just love her, as she is.

Oliver Wendell Holmes once said, "I would not give a fig for the simplicity this side of complexity, but I would give all I possess for the simplicity on the other side of complexity."

As a child I was always busy, rarely spending time alone. The definition of who I was came from doing, not being. I measured myself by the sets of tennis I played, the A's I brought home on my report card, the books I read. The idea of simply being never entered my mind.

Katherine has no wants. She can do nothing. She is defined entirely by her being. Is hers the simplicity on this or the other side of complexity? Perhaps Kat went through the complexity those years she cried every night and felt her brain leaving her. I will never know if Kat felt pain or a terrifying confusion as her neurological system broke down and she lost touch with this world. I will never know whether through the chaos, she achieved peace. When I look at her today—her face smooth and chiseled like a beautiful sculpture, her eyes huge pools of sea—I ask myself, is she a mental castoff or a high spirit holding the secret of life?

Now when I think of Kat's death, a wave of relief sweeps over me. A burden lifts from my shoulders, coupled with a deep loneliness. Without Katherine, who am

I? Kat's silence forced me to look deep within to the very marrow of my being. There I found something I didn't know existed—a love not based on the fulfillment of dreams.

I can't imagine waking up every morning without Katherine in our house. Perhaps her presence will live on without the daily feedings and bathings. Perhaps her essence will remain engraved on my heart.

Years ago, a friend gave me a Christian Dior porcelain box that fits neatly in the palm of my hand. On its gold-embossed top are two leopards stretching gracefully under the green fronds of a palm tree. On the box's base, leopards stalk, quietly guarding the treasure. In the box, I store messages from fortune cookies. I keep those that have, over the years, given me solace and hope. The porcelain box sits on my dresser.

When Kat was small, we often ate at a restaurant called the Mandarin Gardens. Kat sat between Paul and me in the red Naugahyde booth, her eyes glued to the gold dragon hovering over our heads. I've kept the fortunes from those meals.

"Forget the doubts and fears that are creeping into your heart." This was from a meal early on when we'd just noticed changes in Kat, a time of small doubts.

"You will have the fulfillment of a hope." We had by then decided to pattern Kat but had not yet been admitted to the Institutes' program. It, I knew, would provide the cure.

"You will realize your dreams by your own efforts." This fortune appeared during the thick of patterning. I read it daily.

"Your determination will make you succeed in everything." This reinforced what I never doubted.

"There is no grief which time does not lessen and soften." I have come back to this fortune, a harder one to swallow, repeatedly over the years as the pain changed from a constant throb to a series of waves, some larger, some smaller than others.

"Your life is what your thoughts make it." My guide, my wise mentor, this is the fortune I leave on the top of the pile. When I open my magic box, rubbing it gently on its sides, this genie first appears.

"Kat, it has been hard to love you. It has taken me such a long time." I knelt on Kat's mattress on the floor, bending close so my face was a few inches from hers. I'd gotten her off her summer school bus, fed her, brushed her hair, and carried her into her room that July day. She lay on her flowered spread, her head resting against her huge pink bunny.

She looked straight into my eyes, holding every word. She lay still, locking my eyes with hers, and paused silently before her body erupted. She moved her mouth, trying to mold words that wouldn't come. She pushed up

on her arm and bounced back and forth, her elbow bending, a fragile tree blown by a strong wind. She smiled the
most pained smile I have ever seen. She puckered her lips
and moved her tongue from side to side, making nonsense
sounds that spoke louder than words. She'd been waiting
all those years for my words.

I remembered a letter from a friend whose daughter
has Rett syndrome. "Ashley is teaching me so much about
love," he wrote. "She is our love child and our blessing.
For her, I would change her, though sometimes I wonder
if that would be a true help to her. She's as pure love as it
gets, and I treasure being with her." When I'd read his letter, I knew that was where I wanted to be. I knew it could
be done.

I might have been able to kill Katherine gently, quietly in
the womb. If there had been a genetic marker indicating
the tragic life ahead of her, I could have ended it before it
began. She would never have breathed the air, felt the
wind, heard the birds. I might have been able to say, "This
is a life not worth living," before I'd ever known her,
named her, looked into her dark-blue eyes, held her as she
ate from my breast, hugged her as she lay frightened after
a seizure, laughed with her when she giggled at the brilliant colors of Paul's fireworks.

If I'd never known Katherine, I might have been able
to say, "It will be too hard for me, for Paul, for the other

children we'll have. She'll slow us down. She'll be in the way. She'll never be able—no matter how hard she tries—to do anything for herself. This life shouldn't be lived."

Maybe before I met Kat, I could have said that. I could have looked at pictures of other girls with Rett syndrome with their beanpole legs, wringing hands, and distant looks and said, "No, I'd never want a child like that. She has nothing to give. There is no reason for her life."

But I met Kat. I carried her inside me. I carry her outside me. I wrapped her soft body next to mine. I watched her leave me. I could tell she didn't want to, but she couldn't help it. I saw my life shatter. I tried to penetrate her distant world. I tried to grab her back to me. I stopped. I watched. I learned her subtle messages.

Without knowing, over a period of many years, I realized who the real teacher of my life is: the quiet child who asks nothing of me but love. The one who, by her presence, forced me to look inward, who created the reason for the journey, who by doing nothing gave me the push.

Still, there are days when the darkness hits. Some small thing—a babysitter not showing up, the glimpse of a child, now a woman, who was a baby with Kat—puts me over the edge and a leaden weight crushes my heart. I retreat to my bed, bury myself under the covers, and curl into the fetal position I remember so well from the early days with Kat. I'm there again, the sadness paralyzing me, the fear of the future closing around me. I feel myself breaking, all the pieces I'd thought had finally grown strong pulled apart. During those hours of depression, the disintegration feels complete, and I'm certain I've made no progress over the past sixteen years. Then Mark makes me laugh, or a friend calls out of the blue, or the sunset is exquisite, and the pieces I'd thought couldn't be reconstructed fall back into place.

With Kat, I wanted to move on, to find answers and be gone. She stopped me. Like a sharp rock solidly wedged in a streambed, always there as the river flows over it, she taught me about inescapable sorrow. She showed me there are some things we choose in life and some things that choose us.

Quietly, she presented me with the ultimate test. Her deafening question rang in my ears year after year. Sometimes I tried to ignore it, to act as if it and she weren't there. But it always was, and she waited patiently for me to respond to it: Did I have it in me to love without dreams—to love simply for the sake of love with no look to the future, no promises given, nothing expected in return?

A blackbird walks alone on the porch railing as I feed Kat. A loner, it walks back and forth, going through the motions, going nowhere. Kat spits applesauce on the floor.

I sponge it up and go back to feeding her. I look out again and see the blackbird facing me, but this time I see the brilliant iridescent purple, blue, and green of its chest, wild and shocking. I stand stunned, watching its feathers fluff and its colors glisten in the sunlight.

EPILOGUE

PHOTO BY PAUL PHILLIPS

Katherine with her blue doll, spring 1980.

An ancient piñon tree grows from a rock ledge in this desert canyon. Gnarled and gray, on first glance it appears dead. Yet a young branch, strong and elegant, rises from its core. The tree is exquisite. It has learned to let a portion of itself die to allow new growth.

JULY 2003: I sit below Jack Creek Rapid in the depths of Desolation Canyon. The Green River rushes by in a healthy flow after last year's drought conditions, when we spent too much time dragging the raft off sandbars and getting stuck on exposed boulders. The sky is desert blue. Paul and I are alone, our first voyage on the river without children. They are spread around the globe: Helen in Buenos Aires on a grant to study the political underpinnings of the tango; Alice in Guatemala, volunteering at a school; Mark in Costa Rica, studying Spanish, and living with a family. Even Kat is in Florida with Donna, her friend and companion, visiting Donna's daughters.

I never thought I would get to this place of freedom and gratitude. I wrote *Grief Dancers* ten years ago. Though I have written three books since, *Grief Dancers* remains the one book I *had* to write. The process of writing it allowed my heart to mend. And with the mending came a deep appreciation for Katherine: the power of her smile, the strength of her innocence.

A couple of years ago, Kat got very sick. Dehydration, flu—we didn't know what was wrong. One look at Kat in the crowded emergency room waiting area, and they moved her to the front of the line, then rushed her away to start tests. An old woman moaning in the cubicle next to ours was moved out. A man in green scrubs wheeled in a clean bed, quickly occupied by a black man who complained, "Pain in chest, can't breathe." The hustling, bustling, and beeping covered smells of sweat and excrement. Instead of the usual wringing, Kat's hands rested in a peaceful prayer pose. A nurse poked her thin pale arm for blood, inserted an IV, covered her face with an oxygen mask, talked about more tests after X-rays. After two days of hacking coughs, vomiting, and fever, Kat let them do everything without a whimper.

It was 3:00 AM by the time Katherine was transferred from the ER to a regular double. "She might be contagious. We'll close the room," the nurse said with a wink. "You're a saint," I replied. Once Kat was settled in her bed, I fell into the other, squeezing in a couple hours of sleep amid the chattering of equipment and nurses' interruptions.

All the old memories returned, but gently, no longer an eruption. They didn't dredge up the feelings of anguish that doctors and hospital visits once did. Kat is Kat is Kat. Now we weren't waiting for a life diagnosis, but a diagnosis of disease. We'd had the life diagnosis—Rett syndrome—for fifteen years. Despite its crippling ways, Kat had a good life, too good a life to let go of so soon.

The X-rays showed fluid in the lungs—pneumonia. I'd read enough obituaries in the International Rett Syndrome Association newsletter to know that pneumonia is a quick and silent killer. I had the grim realization that Kat will die someday and when she goes, it will be swift, unexpected.

Kat couldn't eat or drink. Everything she took was through tubes. She rested like a spirit, caught somewhere between this life and the next. There wasn't much I could do for her except swab her dry mouth with a peppermint sponge, stay near her to let her know she wasn't alone, and explain to each new nurse who appeared that "she can't talk, can't tell us what's wrong or how she feels, can't do much of anything" and wanting to add, "But look at how beautiful and gentle she is. Isn't that enough in this life, to just be?"

When Donna, the woman who lives with us and helps care for Kat, came down to spell me, she brought a big canvas bag. At home, I took a walk, bathed, ate a bowl of fruit. By the time I returned to Kat's hospital room, it had been transformed. "He's Got the Whole World in His Hands" played from Donna's portable tape deck. Kat's head lay on a flowered pillowcase, ringed by stuffed bears and bunnies. Donna had tacked Christmas lights to the wall where Kat could see them flickering on and off. "I told them she needed to feel like she was at home. I got permission for the lights after they were up," Donna chortled.

On the sixth day, we brought Kat home. By then she ate a little. Her fever was low-grade and her cough less pronounced. We had a megadose of antibiotics to get down her and a suction machine to clear out the mucus. For two weeks, she was listless. The third week, her appetite improved. By the fourth week, she ate with gusto. By the fifth, she smiled that trusting smile of hers. By the sixth week, she was as good as ever.

The seventh week, Donna said, "Well, I think this baby is ready for a trip. Hey Kat, let's go to Canada. We can visit my niece in Manitoba." The eighth week, Donna packed Kat (and the microwave, coffeemaker, Kat's favorite foods, stuffed animals, suitcases) in her van and they were off to Winnipeg, Kat's smile plastered on her face.

"We don't know how long we'll have this precious girl," Donna said as she pulled out of the driveway. "We've gotta do things while we can."

The Green flows past on its never-ending journey. Across the river, red rock cliffs rise a thousand feet. The mosquitoes are biting. I wear a layer of Off and long underwear in an effort to frustrate their hunger.

What is Kat's message? This river's? It's so simple: What is, is. One hundred and forty million years ago, dinosaurs ruled this land. Yesterday, we saw their remains at Dinosaur National Monument. A flood surprised the giants, tossed them down the river to a gully where they were trapped and clustered for all time, until 1909 when paleontologist Earl Douglass dug up a few bones and kept digging, ultimately unearthing the largest fossil find in recorded history. This country speaks in dinosaur time, and I find solace in this immutable land of red rock canyons and rivers that flow through wars, crises, births, and deaths. What is, is.

Five years ago, we converted part of our basement into a small apartment and added a forty-foot wheelchair ramp. Kat lives there with Donna, a sixty-two-year-old dynamo who has opened my eyes to Kat's gifts and goodness. I often tell friends I have two angels in my house. Donna reads scripture to Kat in the mornings, makes vats of soup to take down to a shelter for the homeless, bakes banana bread to give out at the nursing home for her old lady friends, decorates Kat's room with year-round Christmas lights, and tacks stuffed animals to the walls and ceiling. Over Kat's bed is a picture of the family, handmade valentines to Kat from my friend Kate, a clock that plays Christmas tunes on the hour. Donna and Kat have made road trips to San Diego, Mexico, Santa Fe, Ohio, Florida, and Canada. Once or twice a year, they head off and Donna calls periodically to fill me in about the zoos they visit and the friends and relatives they stay with. "Kat's my favorite traveling companion," Donna says. "We like the same music and I never have to make conversation with Kat."

Katherine came close to destroying my life. Or I came close to letting my reaction to Katherine destroy my life. There were times when I knew I couldn't make it. There would be no flavor in my life, just a blandness born of sorrow. But then I had so much to live for: Helen, Alice, Mark, Paul, good friends, nature's glory. Perhaps most of all I had Kat to live for. It just took me a while to figure that out.

Kat has not spoken a word in twenty-four years. Yet she has been our family's primary teacher. Her presence—a touchstone to what is important—has molded us. Perhaps it's because the other children knew if Paul and I stuck by Kat, we'd stick by them through thick and thin. Perhaps it's because the extent of Kat's handicap put everything in perspective and they learned not to sweat the small stuff. So, when Helen developed the hair loss condition alopecia areata and began losing her hair when she was ten, she felt a deep loss, but knew her loss was relative. Today, at twenty-two, she is a senior at Yale, editor of the *Yale Literary Magazine,* fluent in Spanish and Portuguese, and bald and beautiful. Alice is a sophomore at Yale, an outdoor enthusiast who was an instructor on the wilderness orientation program for freshmen. Mark is a junior in high school, National Merit scholar contender, and a budding rock star who found his true voice once he picked up a guitar.

This is our sixth time down this stretch of river. We've been here in lightning, hail, flooding. We've slept under a cascade of stars on still nights and we've been awakened by thunder as a storm turned our campsite into a raging stream. There are moments when the morning sun turns

the red cliffs silver or the night sky blesses us with a shooting star that sings across the galaxies. We've had the best
and the worst on this river, and we keep coming back.

We're at the Butler Rapid campsite now, one of our
favorites. It's a fitting last-night camp, five miles from the
takeout, with a long beach and a mammoth cottonwood
whose branches extend like welcoming arms, providing
shade and protection from the desert wind. Our trip,
ninety miles down one of the few remaining stretches of
wilderness river in the Lower Forty-eight, is coming to a
close. We've had 110-degree heat, windstorms that coated
our food supply with grit, deerflies that bit like hypoder-
mic needles, mosquitoes that have left welts up and down
my legs.

Today the sun burned mercilessly. We hopped in and
out of the river to cool off. The canyon walls seemed
harsh, dried up. Tonight we're sitting on this beach and
the same sun that blazed all day, sapping our energy, is
giving us a light show that brings out every contour, crag,
and color of each butte, throws a streak of gold across the
Green River, illuminates a distant canyon so that it burns
copper and then shines chartreuse. I would suffer any
hardship—and I have—for this half hour, sitting, watching the setting sun play a farewell symphony.

There is a connection between this moment and
Katherine's smile, a deep and certain connection. There
are moments of glory that are worth any sacrifice, any

pain, any struggle, to obtain. Kat's smile, a desert sunset. Somehow they're the same and I would do anything— again and again and again—to experience the joy that both bring.

September 2003: It took me a long time to realize that my parents' difficulty in dealing with Kat stemmed from their own grief. Double grief. They mourned the loss of a healthy grandchild and the loss of a good life for me. They wanted to protect me from those losses but were powerless to do so. They worried that Katherine would take attention away from the other children and would leave me broken and embittered. Over the years, as the other children grew up to be bright and resilient, they grew to appreciate Kat and opened their hearts to her.

My dad died two weeks ago. He was diagnosed with leukemia in January 2002. Both of his parents had lived to be over ninety-five. We were convinced he'd be one of the lucky few who could manage the disease. But his proved to be a rare and stubborn strain. During his last year and a half he traveled to Egypt, Austria, the Czech Republic, Hungary, Costa Rica, Guatemala, Canada, and throughout the States. He played tennis until the May before his death. When he could no longer play tennis, he began writing his memoirs. Never did I hear him complain.

On August 27, Paul and I flew to North Carolina for a visit. Several years before, my parents had sold their rambling New Hampshire house and moved to an elegant, low-maintenance town house in Brevard, about forty minutes from where Mother had been raised in Asheville. My sister was already there. August 28 was my fifty-second birthday, the first birthday I'd shared with my parents in more than thirty years. Dad ate his usual bowl of Grape-Nuts, drank his coffee as he read the newspaper, and drove himself to the hospital five minutes away for his weekly blood transfusion. I joined him at the hospital for lunch, and we spent a couple of hours looking at pictures from a recent trip to Africa, his favorite place. As a parting gift he'd sent the whole family (sixteen of us) to Zimbabwe, Namibia, and Botswana. We'd been back for just a couple of weeks. Until a month before our departure, we'd thought he'd come with us, but there was no way to arrange for blood transfusions in that part of the world. Late in the afternoon, friends stopped by and he rustled up some martinis. That evening, we ate a birthday dinner of gingered pork, squash soup, almond cake with raspberry sauce, and red wine from Montepulciano, Italy. We talked about how we were all looking forward to congregating at their house for Thanksgiving. The next morning Dad woke with a bad headache. Several hours later he was unconscious. My brother, a longtime folksinger, flew in from New Hampshire in time to play Dad his favorite Dylan and Ian and Sylvia tunes. Early in the morning on August 30, he died in his own bed surrounded by the people he loved most.

His memorial service was on September 2, 2003. It was Katherine's twenty-fourth birthday. It was as if she shared her birthday as a sign that she was with him. Now his death and her birth are forever linked, and my birthday and Katherine's have become the bookends of my father's last days.

When I am lonely, when I feel life's emptiness creeping in, I go to Kat's room and snuggle in her bed. I hug Katherine and tell her that I know she understands. I stroke her arm or forehead until all the tension in her crippled body drains from her and she is calm, like a tree whose roots sink to the bedrock of life. I watch her face as I speak, the quick smiles, the searching eyes, the shocking beauty of her innocence. Kat thrust herself helpless upon the world and the world responded with a huge embrace that took me years to see. When I feel the house's silence crashing upon me, Kat soothes away my cares and reminds me that love is enough. No, love is all.

We are our stories. Each story is a ripple that adds to the richness of the larger pool of stories. When we tell our stories, we come to realize that ours is part of something grander than we'd ever imagined. When we share our stories, our pain is released into a huge sea with no boundaries.

ABOUT RETT SYNDROME

Rett syndrome was first described in 1965 by Viennese doctor Andreas Rett in a German medical publication. It was not until 1983 that the first article written about it in English appeared in a widely read neurology journal. Rett syndrome is a unique neurodevelopmental disorder that is found primarily in females but can be seen rarely in males. The disorder results from a mutation in the MECP2 gene on the X chromosome. Prominent features are apparent normal development until between six and eighteen months, followed by a period of regression, which leads to cognitive delay, loss of purposeful hand use, and other developmental deficiencies.

About the Author

Susan Zimmermann is the author of *Writing to Heal the Soul*, winner of the Colorado Book Award, and *Grief Dancers*, a Colorado Book Award finalist. She is the coauthor of *7 Keys to Comprehension* and *Mosaic of Thought*, educational bestsellers that are changing the way reading is taught in classrooms throughout America. A graduate of the University of North Carolina at Chapel Hill and Yale Law School, Susan cofounded and served as the executive director of Denver's Public Education and Business Coalition. A noted speaker and workshop leader, Susan speaks throughout the United States and internationally on ways to deepen reading and writing experiences for adults and children. She lives in the foothills west of Denver with her husband, Paul Phillips, and their four children.

Also by Susan Zimmermann:

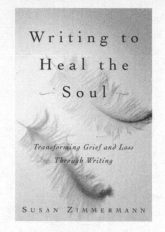

Writing to Heal the Soul
0-609-80829-X
$13.00 paperback

Faced with her daughter's disability, Susan Zimmermann used writing to help herself overcome fear, denial, guilt, bitterness, and despair. *Writing to Heal the Soul* is Susan's gift to others—everyone, not just writers—who are suffering any kind of grief or loss. It offers simple yet inspiring writing exercises to help you transform sadness into acceptance and even joy.

"[Susan's] book is that rare thing, a beautifully written guide-book, both useful and lyrical, pragmatic and poetic."

—MARTHA BECK, author of *Expecting Adam* and
Finding Your Own North Star

AVAILABLE FROM THREE RIVERS PRESS WHEREVER BOOKS ARE SOLD
CROWNPUBLISHING.COM